MW01487264

MONEY MINDSET
SHIFT.
Church Edition

The **Top 9 Myths**
That Keep Christians Stuck Financially and
How To Get Unstuck, Live Debt Free and Build Wealth!

TOYIN CRANDELL

JEREMIAH HOUSE PUBLISHING
Toronto, Ontario

Published in Toronto, Ontario, Canada by Jeremiah House Publishing.

Unless otherwise noted, all Scripture quotations are from the New American Standard Bible, copyright 1960, 1962, 1963, 1968, 1971, 1972, 1973, 1975, 1977 by the Lockman Foundation. Used by permission.

Scripture quotations marked NKJV are taken from the New King James Version. Copyright 1982 by Thomas Nelson, Inc. Used by permission.

Scriptures marked ESV are taken from the Holy Bible, English Standard Version (ESV): Copyright© 2001 by Crossway, of Good News Publishers. Used by permission.

Any italicization or words in brackets added to scripture quotations are the author's addition for emphasis or clarity.

Organizations, churches, pastors and small group leaders can receive special discounts when purchasing this book and other Jeremiah House Publishing resources. For more information, please email info@jeremiahhousepublishing.com

Crandell, Toyin, 1988-, author

Money Mindset SHIFT. Church Edition : The Top 9 Myths That Keep Christians Stuck Financially and How To Get Unstuck, Live Debt Free and Build Wealth! / Toyin Crandell.

ISBN 978-1-989066-04-1 (hardcover)
ISBN 978-1-989066-05-8 (paperback)
ISBN 978-1-989066-06-5 (epub)

Business & Money: Business Culture: Motivation & Self-Improvement
Religion & Spirituality: Christian Living: Business & Professional Growth

DISCLAIMER AND LIMIT OF LIABILITY: While anyone may find the teachings, practices, disciplines, techniques, examples, and anecdotes in this book to be useful, this book is sold with the understanding that neither the author nor Toyin Crandell Coaching are engaged in presenting any specific financial, tax, career, legal, psychological, emotional, or health advice. Nor is anything in this book an analysis, recommendation, solution, diagnosis, prognosis, or cure for any specific career, financial, psychological, emotional, or health circumstance or problem. Every person has unique needs and circumstances and this book does not take those individual needs and circumstances into account. Any person experiencing financial or career concerns, or any anxiety, depression, stress, health, or relationship issues, should consult with a financial or tax advisor, career counselor, medical doctor, licensed psychologist, licensed therapist, or other appropriate qualified professional before commencing any new financial plan or transaction, career strategy, change in personal relationships, exercise program, or following any of the teachings, methods, and suggestions described in this book. This book is not a substitute for the reader enlisting qualified professionals to assist with the reader's specific circumstances, issues and problems.

Printed In Canada

I would like to dedicate this book to my Father (Abba), my Lord and Saviour Jesus Christ, and my sweet friend, Holy Spirit. Thank You for Your consistent guidance, wisdom and written Word.

I also dedicate this book to every coach and mentor who has believed in and poured into me whether in a business context or casual conversation. You changed my life. You changed the lives of each person my message reaches.

But if any of you lacks wisdom, let him ask of God, who gives to all generously and without reproach, and it will be given to him.
James 1:5

CONTENTS

INTRODUCTION

This book is my account of how I shifted from tens of thousands of dollars in debt, unable to earn enough to buy food for our family and totally broke in my mindset to building a wealth mindset and then reality, while remaining firmly planted in the love of God and His Son Jesus Christ.

It is a manual to help Christians called to the workplace as career professionals and business owners identify and address the top nine myths that keep you stuck, stagnant or simply left your potential dormant. These myths have kept Christians in struggle and self-focus, unable to freely support the work of spreading the gospel to every nation on the earth.

In light of this, the book has been divided into three parts. The first is a needed conversation about money. After years of money being the unspoken, despised, ignored but much needed resource in the Body, we are going to look at it for exactly what it is. We will discuss its purpose and why Christians who are called and capable of building wealth should.

Part Two is our Myth Analysis. This is where we will identify the top nine myths, specific to Christians which hold you back from fulfilling your potential in the workplace and in business.

Finally, in Part Three, we will discuss exactly what you need to do to get unstuck, live debt free and build wealth.

I advise you to take the time to read this book through, and keep it as a go-to when the mindset roadblocks discussed re-surface. Changing how you think and therefore live is not a one shot job. It takes months and years of conditioning, bible study and practice.

Get another copy of this book as a lifeline for anyone you may know at their wits' end, trying to figure out what is keeping them in negative financial patterns. Give this book to Christians who want to transition from an uncertain job market to being their own boss. And also for those who may not be Christian, but are spiritual and have fallen prey to some of these mindsets, help them break free as well.

This is also a valuable resource for finance coaches and counsellors, Pastors and parents (biological and spiritual) with advice to help those in your care desperately trying to change their financial situation but not knowing what is keeping them stuck.

My goal is to see one million people set free financially so that they can freely and without worry, fulfill their purpose and do what they have been placed on this planet for.

And I want you to be one of them. So pick up your journal and a pen and set your heart to learn.

To your financial freedom,

Toyin C.

BEFORE WE BEGIN
Do Not Blame Your Pastor

Frankly, too many people are quick to blame pastors for every gap they see in the Body of Christ. Pastors are often expected to be experts in every single subject and able to save you from making bad spiritual, practical, mental, material, relational decisions. They are expected to do all of this while visiting those who are sick in the hospital, praying for the congregation, evangelising, bringing in new converts, preparing spirit filled sermons and the list goes on. It's unrealistic. Your pastor is not responsible for your financial future, you are.

A reason why many pastors do not teach on this subject is because when they do, they are criticized for not focusing on spiritual things. Some people tune out the pastor as soon as he or she mentions money, thinking that his or her entire focus is in taking their tithe. So even if pastors wanted to speak about this, many are ignored or criticized.

The body of Christ needs various experts to step up and teach one another what we know. I encourage pastors to invite financial experts to speak with your members so that the matter is no longer a taboo conversation. It doesn't have to be in the context of a Sunday service, but as a practical breakout session to meet the needs of the people.

We need the people of God to break out of the lack cycle and move in the fullness of what God intended for us. The intent of this book is to help Christians in every denomination do better financially; because when you thrive, the church, our missionaries, God projects and the gospel of the Kingdom thrives with you.

PART ONE

THE MONEY CONVERSATION

That our sons may be as plants grown up in their youth;
That our daughters may be as pillars, sculptured in palace style;

That our barns may be full, supplying all kinds of produce;
That our sheep may bring forth thousands and ten thousands in our fields;

That our oxen may be well laden;
That there be no breaking in or going out;
That there be no outcry in our streets.

Happy are the people who are in such a state;
Happy are the people whose God is the Lord!

Psalm 144:12-15 (NKJV)

CHAPTER 1

My Story:
Moving From Struggle To Significance

Growth is painful. Change is painful. But, nothing is as
painful as staying stuck where you do not belong.

— Narayana Murthy

_____

10 years ago, I amassed tens of thousands of dollars worth
of "stupid" debt. I had racked this up during university,
even though my educational expenses were covered by scholarships. Essentially, I ran a painting business that had $150,000
total in revenue, then proceeded to spend that plus much,
much more, trying to impress those around me. I was stuck
for years and never thought I could come out of that debt. I
finally had a mindset breakthrough and paid it off within 2
years while earning barely enough to pay it off.

Fast forward to a few years after paying off the debt, I
continued to live in financial struggle. After getting married

and having my first child, I took a leap from working a traditional job and made the transition to entrepreneurship. Little did I know this would expose just how *off* I was with money. Six months into my entrepreneurial journey things had gone from tight to unimaginable. At this time, my husband and I were renting a 700 square foot basement apartment. Without a steady paycheck to fall back on, we began to seriously discuss going to the food bank because there was no food in our house.

I remember that night in December like it was yesterday. Things that week were just "a bit tight" in my perspective and my husband, Joshua had been making canned food for me all week long. We were grateful and thanking God that we could feed our baby breastmilk and not have to worry about how she would eat. I then asked him what he had been eating, since he hadn't eaten with me all week, which was our norm. He responded that his dinner had been some chocolates we received for Christmas that month. I was shocked. He said, "we need to go to the food bank. There's literally nothing left."

That was my wake up call.
My business was not working.
Something was wrong with our finances.
Seriously wrong.

It would have been different if we had not learned anything about personal finances, had not read a large number of books dealing with personal finances and had no access to the internet and the wealth of information it provides. But we lived in North America, surrounded by opportunity and access to many of the resources we needed.

There was no excuse. I knew that God did not give us access to so much to continue in this way despite all our work.

I knew that I did not want to raise my daughter in a place of uncertainty about her basic needs. I also knew that I could not help others encounter the freedom that is within the kingdom of God if our finances were suffering so severely we didn't earn enough to buy food.

For about a year leading up to that point, the Holy Spirit had given me this prayer, "Abba, change the way I think." I had been praying it consistently because I knew there was something amiss but did not know how much. Once I started to pray this, it led to a season where Abba asked me to take a leap of faith and pursue "full-time ministry". From my perspective, that meant full-time evangelistic efforts: preaching, running Bible studies, worship leading and the like. For 3 years, I had been doing this sort of ministry: pursuing evangelistic efforts for 7 months out of the year and working part-time for the remaining 5 months. I thought He simply wanted me to transition to doing the same thing 12 months straight.

I was very hesitant. My current ministry and work schedule left me in financial lack almost all the time. The 5 months in which I would work, I was doing so much ministry work concurrently that it was not quite part-time hours. The hours never made enough to cover my bills. Years before, I also tried asking Christian brothers and sisters for support to cover me while I focused on ministry work. That had failed miserably resulting in me almost getting evicted from my apartment.

After that experience, I was disappointed. I didn't want to lean on the Body for financial help because I felt that most of the sincere believers around me were in similar positions. They would give what they could, but it had not proved enough to sustain me when I was single, much less now, being married with a little daughter to care for.

So I turned to God and said, "Abba, I'll do it. I'll do full-time ministry, but I need you to help me. I need you to help me set myself up financially to do this for decades without burning out because of lack."

I watched many people called to this form of ministry start with great zeal. But after 5 years of not having the finances to keep their family afloat, they would often give up and go back to whatever they were doing previously. And these were gung-ho, highly motivated, all or nothing people! If they turned back from the financial pressure of mission work, I knew I would not make it if I didn't have a plan.

My heart burned to be a financial pillar who could pour into those who are called and help to sustain the work of God in different spheres of society. But before I could help anyone else, I knew I needed to be able to help myself.

MY TIME OF PREPARATION

I asked God to teach and prepare me for the place of ministry He was calling me into and decided to read 50 books in 6 months as part of my "School of the Spirit" (a self-learning curriculum I had been practicing for years). I also decided to sit with missionaries who had been successful in their work long-term, as well as speak with successful business owners who loved Jesus Christ, in order to learn about finances from them.

The first book I read was *Fully Funded Missionary* by Rob Parker and before I had completed Chapter One, I was rocked. Rob Parker highlighted that many Christians going into missions work were not facing the financial responsibility head on and did not have a plan in place to build a strong support network and partnership team for the journey. They figured God would just take care of it, which left them prey to quitting before their time. Right off the bat, he challenged his readers to examine what they believed about God and money and to see if it was from the Word of God or simply tradition, stories and general church sentiment.

I put the book down and asked the Lord to show me what I personally believed about money that was not biblical. I felt the Holy Spirit gave me point after point. As I wrote them down, I asked, "What on earth could be *wrong* with these beliefs? These statements are true!"

I believed things like, "If I have a need, I should pray and ask God, not people, and He will speak to men on my behalf," or that, "Raising financial support is contrary to having faith." Even more, I believed that the more uncertainty my financial present or future had, the more faith I must have in God.

And God began to challenge me on each point with specific scriptures and stories from His Word. For example, concerning asking people directly for financial assistance, He sent me to Matthew 7:7-8:

"Ask, and it will be given to you; seek, and you will find; knock, and it will be opened to you. For everyone who asks receives, and he who seeks finds, and to him who knocks it will be opened."

I protested and said but Abba, I *do* ask, I ask *You*!

Joseph Asked The Butler

He then sent me to Genesis 40 and the story of Joseph. Joseph had been unjustly thrown into Pharaoh's prison and in his time there, he had been promoted by the Warden for his leadership and assistance with other inmates. He happened to interpret a dream for the Pharaoh's chief butler which prophesied that the butler would be restored to the palace. When he made this interpretation, he specifically asked,

"Only keep me in mind when it goes well with you, and please do me a kindness by mentioning me to Pharaoh and get me out of this house. For I was in fact kidnapped from the land of the Hebrews, and even here I have done nothing that they should have put me into the dungeon."

Genesis 40:14-15.

After interpreting the dream, Joseph didn't just pray and ask God that the chief butler would remember him when he was restored to Pharaoh's house. He asked the man directly.

I was paying attention.

Esther Asked The King

Next, God led me to the story of Esther. Queen Esther was a Jewish woman who had been taken by King Ahasuerus as a slave and then made into the Queen of Persia. During her time in the Palace, Haman, one the King's top aides determined to destroy the Jewish people. He schemed and got permission from the King to destroy all the Jews in the land on a specific day. While repealing this death verdict might have been risky or almost impossible, Queen Esther was the only one with access to the King and a vague chance of changing his mind.

Esther asked that all the Jewish people in the province would pray and fast with her for 3 days. Her request was not for God to speak to the King in a dream instructing him to protect her people. No, she prayed, fasted then approached the King *directly* and asked that her life and the lives of her people would be spared. See Esther 7:2-4.

Nehemiah Asked The King

As if that was not enough, Abba then sent me to the story of Nehemiah. Nehemiah was serving in a foreign King's palace when he heard about the destruction that had taken place in Jerusalem. He was crushed and it showed on his face while working.

"So the king said to me, "Why is your face sad though you are not sick? This is nothing but sadness of heart." Then I was very much afraid. I said to the king, "Let the king live forever. Why should my face not be

sad when the city, the place of my fathers' tombs, lies desolate and its gates have been consumed by fire?" Then the king said to me, "What would you request?" **So I prayed to the God of heaven. I said to the king, "If it please the king, and if your servant has found favor before you, send me to Judah, to the city of my fathers' tombs, that I may rebuild it"... I also said to the king, "If it please the king, let me have letters addressed to the governors of the province west of the Euphrates River, instructing them to..." And the king granted these requests, because the gracious hand of God was on me."** Nehemiah 2:1-5, 7-8.

So when Nehemiah was faced with what looked like an impossible challenge, he prayed and fasted, but he didn't stop there. When given an opportunity to ask, he didn't respond with an "I'll just wait for the Holy Spirit to tell you". No, he asked for what he needed. Then, once his initial request was granted, he asked for what he would need to further accomplish the mission successfully.

This was only one of about seven key beliefs I had written down and firmly agreed with. Through this experience, He started showing me how I had built much of my beliefs about God and money on church tradition and stories I had heard from others, not the Bible itself.

The more I studied in this season, the more I knew that transforming lives financially was the "ministry" He had been calling me to. This was when the real battle between my beliefs about money as a Christian and the truth began. I had already taught and assisted people with debt freedom, with a focus on practical strategies they could use but there was more to the picture.

I realized I had conflicting desires. I believed that I had more faith while in financial struggle and that the hardship made me feel as though my walk with God was closer. I also believed that if I had excess money, it would negatively affect my relationship with God and that was and will always be my highest priority.

So you can guess what happened. I did what many Christian entrepreneurs do. I ran a very expensive hobby instead of a profitable business. I was subconsciously unwilling to have profit so I avoided charging what I was worth. I felt guilty about having money come in, though I was happy to have almost or "just enough" to cover my expenses. My internal beliefs kept my family stuck in financial struggle and I could not understand what was happening. I previously thought us being debt-free was the same as financially free but I had now subconsciously brought my income to just below our expenses.

At the same time, I was learning more about money and business than I ever had before. I had opportunities to be coached by some of the most phenomenal Christian mentors, many of whom were multi-millionaires from different countries, backgrounds and business sectors.

I started to notice how different my way of thinking was from theirs. While I felt guilty about not doing purely evangelistic work because I was running a business, they recognized running their businesses well was worship to God.

My Mindset Had to Change

One day I was sitting with a friend in these new circles and a woman complimented me on the boots I was wearing. I responded "Oh, this? I got it for $5 bucks from Ardenes!" She looked at me like I had two heads. Though she just awkwardly smiled and then looked away, her expression asked me "Why on earth did you tell me that?". I realized that the struggle mindset was much deeper than I thought.

I was used to comparing my level of lack with other Christian friends. If someone complimented me or another person on something, we were quick to remove any value from it so that we didn't appear to be wasting money on worldly things. "I just got it from the dollar store," or, "Oh this? It's my sister's, I borrowed it." Once again, I was alarmed by my own thinking.

Soon after, I joined a leadership program led by Jim Foster with Transformation Canada. In order to get started, we needed to do a corporate leadership assessment and speak to an expert to assess our strengths and weaknesses. The assessment was extremely detailed with over 200 questions. In my conversation with the consultant, he very accurately detailed my strengths and potential. He said something that caught my attention. "Toyin, you have a very unique profile. With the balance of your EP, AP, IP and Emotional Quotient," this sounded like blah blah blah to me, "You have the ability to impact people globally. But I can see two reasons you may never do that."

The first part of what he said was in line with *many* prophecies I had received over the years from established men and women of God but the second half? This guy had my attention. I asked him what are the weaknesses that would hold me back. He said, "You are very much motivated by service and people," to which I enthusiastically agreed. "However, you are almost *de*motivated by money." Since I now have a better understanding of where my brain was, I can rephrase that:

I was afraid of money.

Why did this matter? He continued to speak candidly, "In order for you to reach the number of people you are capable of reaching and impacting positively, you will have to be comfortable with setting financial goals and hitting them. Money will have to pass through your hands and you have to be okay with that. Right now, you're not."

I confirmed this to be true because, over that year, my husband had commented on my unprofitable business practices.

- *Never* following up on unpaid invoices.
- Giving my services for free again and again.
- Spending time earmarked for the business helping everyone and their friend.
- Avoiding difficult conversations.
- The list goes on...

I was really bothered by this discovery not because I cared about the money (as you can see, that was the least of my worries). I was concerned because I *knew* that I was placed on this planet to transform lives and draw people closer to the truth of God and His word. Part of that calling was through my business. If I was sabotaging my own business because of the fear of money, I was putting *money* above *God's* calling on my life. For me, that was unacceptable.

A few days later, I was at the same Leadership Edge program sitting in a hotel conference room with other emerging Leaders being trained by Glem Dias. Glem Dias is an amazing Leadership Architect who has served various Fortune 500 companies, training their top directors and CEOs on leadership. He drew a diagram for us: see page 25.

He asked each of us to indicate where we were on this chart. At that time, I was between struggle and survival. He then asked us where we aspired to be. It was a no brainer for me: significance.

As he continued teaching, I had an "aha" moment. How can I help people out of struggle and into living their purpose if I am still between struggle and survival myself? How can someone who is barely hanging onto a raft pull others out of

The diagram Glem Dias drew for us, October 2017

the dangers of the storm that is drowning them? I needed to learn what was causing this fear of money and holding me back financially on a mental level *pronto*.

I knew what to do. Yet I would do it, see success and then sabotage my progress. That year, I would fluctuate between $7000 in income for some months and barely having enough for our bills in others.

That same month of October in 2017, I sent an email to friends and family asking for financial help because of a specific decision I made to help someone else to the tune of hundreds of USD, which put us behind once again in our own bills. Having to send that email was a second wake up call. I got fed up with my lack mindset. I broke agreement with struggle and committed to changing my mind and financial status so that I could live out God's purpose unhindered.

THE FRUIT OF MY MINDSET SHIFT

At the beginning of November, around my birthday, I created a program to retrain my own mind and way of thinking. I spent honest, grueling time with the Lord writing down even more unhealthy financial beliefs that I had. I also put together exercises to help me dig deeper than the surface and find hidden beliefs that were chaining me to lack. I compiled all the lessons I had learned over the years from these millionaire mentors and wrote down what I noticed about how they looked at God and money.

When the month of November ended, my husband reviewed my business numbers and said to me, "Toyin... what happened? Last month, we didn't have enough for our bills. This month you earned more than you did all of last *year*. In one month! What happened?" I said to him, "I've changed how I think."

I was set free to earn and save enough to take care of my family as well as others in the body of Christ. I was able to sponsor projects that Abba has called me to and to give without regretting it afterward. My mindset had completely shifted and I was set free to trust God with my life financially.

The results were so spectacular, I was so different internally, that I wondered if this program and system would help my clients as well. I was teaching them how to be debt free and giving other clients strategies to increase their income. However, I noticed that while 60% of my clients applied what they were learning, about 40% would receive these amazing strategies for changing their financial destiny, but were doing the same thing I was, sabotaging themselves.

Some would have the perfect budget and go right back to their old habits of spending without permanently paying their debt off. They would increase their income by thousands of dollars monthly and still be just as "broke" as they were when they met me. This used to frustrate me immensely.

I introduced my clients to the exercises and activities I created in November 2017. I committed to never again give budgets or strategy without helping people get their mind right first. I watched our success rate go from 60% to about 99%.

Now, I refuse to coach anyone who does not go through our foundational *Money Mindset SHIFT.* program. Finding out your money mindset roadblocks and getting them cleared is paramount to going from being stuck, to thriving financially and in every other area of your life.

MY MISSION

I started off totally unaware of where this journey would lead. I have no business degree or innate smarts. I studied biology at university. Both of my parents are career professionals. I am now a Dave Ramsey Solutions Master Financial Coach as well as a certified Neuroscience Coach and Leader specializing in Entrepreneurship, Health, Relationships, Spirituality and Education. I have coached thousands of people in Canada and the USA in our in-person and online workshops. We have helped hundreds of clients pay off almost a million dollars worth of debt in the last 3 years and increase their incomes and net worth by hundreds of thousands of dollars. While helping others change their lives and families, our business has gone from zero dollars in revenue to multiple six figures.

Am I perfect? No.

Do I work hard enough? Probably not.

Do I have a Ph.D.? Nope!

Am I an intellectual genius? Yes! At least my husband thinks I am.

Was I born with a trust account from my parents to "get me going"? I wish.

God saw my heart, put me through the fire so that I would

always have empathy and compassion for others making the transition from struggle to significance. He then equipped me to shine His light in this area that affects almost every other area of our lives.

When I studied to receive my Neuroscience certification, I was amazed by the wisdom of God. I had already created a program that was firmly backed up by intricate, detailed scientific studies and I didn't even know what the word amygdala was. The certification and study process took my practice up many levels but did not change any of the foundational pieces God had given me that month of November 2017.

Now, I know that many people are committed to struggle, a victim mentality, and unwilling to change their beliefs even when face to face with truth. This book is not for them. This book is for those who have been called to the marketplace and know that this is a space for them to shine the glory, grace, and wisdom of God.

My mission is to help at least 1 million people to take their place as financial pillars in God's kingdom. One million people who will financially back and release churches, missionaries, and young people into their God-given destiny to get souls saved, healed and delivered.

Please notice I didn't say, "If only I could get 1 person to shift, I will be satisfied." Yes, of course I am thankful for every single person who hears these truths and changes their financial trajectory but I *want* to see at least a million people shift.

So why ask for one when I want a million? Because it looks more spiritual and "humble" to do so? I refuse to do that. Jesus died for the entire world. He went to the cross so that billions of people would be saved (2 Pet 3:9). So why do we sit satisfied with one when there are more in need?

Let's get over ourselves, thank God for what we have, and begin to **ask** God for **more**.

ACTIVATION POINT:

- Ask the Holy Spirit, "What are some of the beliefs I have about money that are holding me back?"
- Speak to a trusted friend or significant other about what they have noticed in your financial habits.
- Do an honest assessment of your current financial reality. Earning $10,000 a month doesn't mean you are living out your financial potential. Many people who earn a lot are stuck or comfortable and could be doing more for the kingdom. Give no excuses. Your external reality is a reflection of what is happening internally.
- Write it all down so that you know what needs to change.

CHAPTER 2

Why Money Matters

"Money will do good as well as harm.
In the hands of good men and women it could accomplish,
and it has accomplished, good."

— Russell Conwell

Many people have negative associations with money because they believe that money is the root of many of the evils, disappointments, and challenges they have experienced in life.

Some of us believe that the more money a person has, the farther they must be from having a vibrant relationship with God. Some think that money has the capacity to harden the heart and remove a need for faith in the Christian walk.

Some of us feel that earning money is a distraction from doing the real work of God and that it has the ability to control, change, and corrupt us. We preach against it, judge those who have it and pretend we don't need it.

We despise those, who for the sake of money have caused great harm to others through human trafficking, drug dealing, slavery and the like. Not to mention, we highlight business owners who cheat, embezzle funds or lie for financial gain. Yet...

We pray and ask God for it. Testify when we receive it and are saddened when we lose it.

Those who are called to the marketplace are often made to feel like second class Christians who simply don't have the faith to do the work of the ministry. We treat money as a despised thing, though the physical needs of some brothers and sisters around us are staggering. Even more, some churches are unable to focus on serving the community because they are trying to keep the lights on.

Those who believe that Christians can be wealthy are labeled prosperity while those who believe Christians are meant to be poor and suffer are labeled poverty. For fear of being labeled and isolated, the majority of us say nothing, do nothing and try to avoid the entire conversation.

All the while we watch others live out the calling of God on their lives, take risks, with or without finances and wonder how they can be so... free.

Here's the deal...

MONEY IS NEUTRAL

Money simply reflects what is within the heart of the person who has or does not have it. It's true. Some people have been inspired by money to commit the most atrocious crimes against others. But was it the money that motivated their actions or was what was already in their heart simply amplified when money came into the picture?

When I started learning that money could be used for good, I read *Beyond the Four Walls* by Derek Schneider and came across the story of Pastor Sunday Adelaja. Here is an excerpt:

> He is a Nigerian Pastor of a church in Ukraine with over 25,000 members, (then the largest Evangelical Charismatic church in all of Europe) made up of 99% white people, in the former Soviet Union. Here are some staggering recorded statistics up to 2004 taken from the book 10 Years of Grace that truly reveal the great work God was doing in and through this ministry. The Embassy of God Church was only ten years old by this point; it had begun officially in 1994.
> - Over one million salvations in the first eight years.
> - Over 300 churches planted in over thirty countries.
> - 3000 leaders ministering in the Kiev church.
> - 1000 salvations recorded monthly in the Embassy of God's central church (over 10,000 per year).
> - All night prayer meetings being held nightly along with other strategic prayer initiatives.
> - 1000-2000 people fed daily in the church's *Stephania Soup Kitchen*.
> - Over 3000 people set free from drug and alcohol addiction.
> - Homes for street and abandoned children were established and over 500 children have been restored to their families.
> - A television ministry that reaches over 100 million homes across Europe, Africa, and Russia was established.

- Political and Senate leaders are members of and attend the church regularly.
- Thousands of mafia members have come to Christ.
- The church's hotline has counselled over 70,000 people, of which 1500 are now church members.
- Many schools for ministry and training have been established.
- Hundreds of thousands of Christians work and are impacting all social spheres of life and society.

It is important for me to note that to date these statistics have actually grown and there has been even more increase in the influence of this particular church in Ukraine and throughout the world.[1]

I watched a few of Pastor Sunday's videos and learned that when he started his church they were consistently struggling financially which distracted them from doing the work of the kingdom. He decided he would become a millionaire in USD within two years so that finances were no longer an issue. Through business ventures and passive income streams, he became a millionaire in 9 months. He didn't stop there. He equipped 200 members of his church to become what they called "millionaire missionaries" in the span of 2 years.

Their ability to come out of a place of lack and build wealth as a church wasn't focused on their personal needs but enabled them to become effective for their community. Each of the 70,000 people who utilized their church's counselling services, others who used their rehabilitation centres or their soup kitchen is evidence of this. The church was obedient and set themselves up financially so that they could create these platforms for their community.

To the pure, all things are pure; but to those who are defiled and unbelieving, nothing is pure, but both their mind and their conscience are defiled.

Titus 1:15

If you are weighed down trying to please everyone around you, the way you use money will demonstrate that. If you are insecure in yourself and your abilities, money will reflect that. If you avoid things you don't understand, money will show it. If you want to make your community better, money will reflect that.

Money does not change your heart but simply exposes what has been there all along. If you love Jesus more than anything else, money will be a tool to express your love for Him.

GOD'S WORK REQUIRES MONEY

Outside of watching so many people in churches and doing the work of full-time ministry struggle, I had an experience that really opened my eyes to why it matters to have money for God's work. Some years ago, I was honoured to participate in a robust leadership experience visiting multiple not for profits and assessing their needs, strengths, and weaknesses with a team of fellow leaders. I was the only Christian in the group.

In our assignment, three of the sites we visited were run by hard-working and service-oriented Christian brothers and sisters while various others were run by other non-religious men and women who also deeply cared about their community. These people were all giving their time and effort to make things better for those in need in their various communities.

At the end of our visits, my group debriefed and one person noted that the three sites that impacted the team's heart collectively were the least funded sites. These sites just happened to be the three Christian sites; one of which had our entire team in tears of wonder and gratitude for the way they were serving the disabled.

My colleague said something to the effect of, "I know all the places we visited are doing great work in the communities they're located, but these three stood out. Yet the other locations had so much more funding and are scaling their work, while these guys are struggling to stay open." I had noticed the same thing and was heartbroken. This is God's business. This is God's work.

We have set Christians up to fail financially with a lack of easily accessible biblical and practical teaching on finances. Often when solid teaching is shared, there is an unspoken culture within the church that honours poverty, lack, struggle, and financial dependence while celebrating the other parts of salvation that Jesus died for.

I have noticed over the years that people are much more excited when we pray for and witness a physical healing, mental deliverance or spiritual breakthrough and will even celebrate a *miraculous* financial breakthrough. But when a person simply runs their business profitably, does great work by focusing on their career and becoming the best in their field, we begin to doubt the genuineness of their faith. Yet, we expect them to be able to sponsor church projects, tithe faithfully and give generously. It's a double standard that crushes Christians.

When I share testimonies of praying for a schizophrenic who receives deliverance and is able to get off his medication, it is more celebrated as a work of God, than when I share how a single mom was able to change her thinking and double her income by getting a job that values her time. Even though she no longer works two jobs plus overtime and can now spend time with her child, all of a sudden, some Christians believe this to be unspiritual.

When I made the transition into full-time business and actually began to prosper, I had a few friends sit me down to see if I was "still saved", if I still loved Jesus like I did when I shared about Him on the streets and was ridiculed for the gospel. Some wanted to see if I was still as "on fire" when my business was finally in proper order as when my business was struggling so much I needed to "lean more" on God.

I shared with them testimonies of being able to reach people with the gospel through my business that would never have listened to me on the streets. I shared about those, who by the nature of the *help* I was able to give them, witnessed how these biblical principles worked, were set free from limiting beliefs, grew financially, and received *hope*. Who is the hope I am sharing? It is Christ in me, the hope of glory! A few have seen how real Jesus is that they gave their lives to Him, even though that was not my intention or the focus of the conversation.

In this time of changing how I think and live, I had friends send me messages and social media posts about the "love of money" because in their minds, simply having money or teaching people how to work smart and not just hard was paramount to the pursuit of money.

They haven't been in conversations I have had with fathers and husbands who contemplate *suicide* because they don't know what else to do to provide enough for their families. They don't hear the 72 year old woman who called me to tell me that she wishes she had heard about my teaching decades ago because her life is almost through and all her life, *all her life,* she has given to church, prayed, tithed, paid her bills and remained in debt and poverty not knowing how to get out.

Money matters whether we like it or not; it is an intrinsic part of Western civilization. If a person has all the love in the world, they cannot go to their landlord and pay the rent with it. Love is important. Peace, joy, faith, truth these are all important. Money and the proper use of it are also important. To ignore this would be to set millions up for unnecessary struggle, anxiety, stress and worry during their lifetime.

One of the most frustrating parts of this is, if people do not seek to understand the importance of this, they run the risk of raising children who are also financially bound and run a higher risk of making the same mistakes as their parents.

Money Matters Because... It Can Be Used To Demonstrate The Kingdom Of God

Guess what? Jesus met the felt needs of the people in His day. When He showed up to introduce them to the Kingdom of God, He didn't just preach at them from morning until night. He healed their diseases! He fed them! He ministered to their *physical* needs. By simply telling people to get saved, be healed physically and delivered spiritually, but struggle and suffer materially until you get to heaven is to limit a believer's potential Kingdom impact in the here and now.

It is to encourage them to hope in dying quickly to enjoy God's Kingdom on the other side, instead of seeking to do God's will on earth as it is in heaven (Matthew 6:10). The kingdom is teaching people how to be able to leave an inheritance abundant enough to reach their children's children. That includes teaching their children sound financial principles. Otherwise, any money or inheritance left could be squandered in one generation.

Introducing the kingdom of God to a family that cannot pay their light bill is not just about paying their light bill that month. It is about giving them the tools to use their God-given minds to create income that removes them from poverty *permanently*. That is Kingdom.

MONEY MATTERS BECAUSE... GOOD PEOPLE DO GOOD THINGS WITH MONEY

Christians should take full advantage of the opportunities around us to build wealth ethically and morally because it is a tool to do *good!* I'm not saying that Christians are perfect and make great decisions every time. But if you are reading this book, it is because your inherent desire is to achieve some of these good things:

- Leave a legacy for your children and their children.
- Give extravagantly to deserving projects.
- Spend quality time with your family members without being absent-minded, worrying about how the bills will be paid.
- Giving your time more freely to service projects and missions work.

These good things are not limited to the four mentioned above. I'm not saying that Christian not-for-profits are more deserving of financial support than other not-for-profits. The more people serving those in need, the better. What I am saying is this: Christians by the nature of our belief and what the bible teaches us should be likely to use financial resources in a way that benefits others.

Good people do good things with money. There is an abundance of money in the world, especially in the West. It is available to anyone who is willing to do the work and present value for it. That money is able to make a huge difference all over the world. But we collectively penalize people for having it while demanding that they use it to further God's work.

When Jesus ministered on earth, there were specific women who, *"provided for him out of their substance"* (Luke 8:1-3). He didn't eat food daily through miracles. They had a treasurer and bought food. We hear much teaching on when they caught a net breaking amount of fish but that wasn't their daily experience.

When revival broke out in Jerusalem and thousands were added to the church, they met in houses. People needed to own houses for those meetings to take place. Acts Chapter 4 shares how many sold their lands and houses in order to provide for others in need. If they never had any assets and were all suffering, they would have all been waiting on a miracle to feed the multitudes that were being added daily to the church.

Like one of my mentors says: Money buys bibles, and it pays for missionary outreaches. Money was used to produce that favourite worship album of yours and market it so you could hear about it. Money was used to print this book in your hands which will undoubtedly set millions free to live again.

God's grace is what enables all of this to happen, but He won't step down from heaven to do our part. If the majority of people in the Western church are "broke", stuck in survival mode, and are waiting on the few families that have generational wealth to give when there is a need, what are we saying about our Father in heaven?

MONEY MATTERS BECAUSE… IT OFTEN AFFECTS YOUR ABILITY TO FULLY OBEY GOD

Here's another reason money matters. Be honest in answering this question:

If God told you to leave your country, travel to another and give your life to the work of the gospel right now, could you leave? Or would you be chained down because of your mortgage debt, credit card debt, car loans or financial insecurity?

Here is a piece of humble pie to those who claim that they do not care about money and money doesn't make any difference or effect in their lives. If you cannot make a decision about what God is telling you to do because of the abundance or lack of money, money controls your life. Not Jesus.

Money matters because when it is mishandled and there is not enough, it occupies mental space whether you admit it or not. I have seen God provide for me miraculously time and time again. However, in between those miracles were real, stressed out moments where I could not focus fully on the work He sent me to do because I was busy trying to gather the finances to do it!

Of course, you can simply go where God has sent you and believe He will provide supernaturally, in fact, I've done that myself. But if you are leaving debts behind, it leaves a bad witness to your debtors.

Think about if you transition to a new place to serve the gospel mission. Having money saved and even passive income in place will allow you to focus on the task He sent you to do. You are more able to focus on bringing His kingdom to those in need instead of focusing on how you will feed your family tomorrow. If you are busy worrying about avoiding eviction or shuffling money around so that bills don't bounce, how do you expect to give honest and focused attention, and do so selflessly, to those at your workplace or in your business?

MONEY MATTERS… FOR YOUR FAMILY

But if anyone does not provide for his relatives, and especially for members of his household, he has denied the faith and is worse than an unbeliever.
1 Timothy 5:8 ESV

I remember my dad highlighting this scripture to me in my single years and I was uncomfortable hearing it. It was so contrary to my belief system at that time that "God would provide and I would not need to worry or think about my financial future". Becoming responsible for another human being - my daughter - opened my eyes very quickly.

A good man leaves an inheritance to his children's children, but the sinner's wealth is laid up for the righteous.
Proverbs 13:22 ESV

I have watched people walk away from the faith because their parents did not have any biblical teaching on finances outside of giving to the church. They watched them give all their money away leaving their children without food, clothing, proper shoes or other necessities. These children grew into adults who believed that God cared nothing about them because their parents gave blindly instead of caring for their needs. Their parents either received bad advice or did not take the time nor make the sacrifices necessary to learn about how money works. It is a hard pill to swallow but we need to wake up!

I am not saying this to condemn anyone but to show you how important this is.

Money Matters Because... Debt Is Unbiblical

Without getting into the nitty-gritty details of good versus bad debt, let us discuss the concept of debt. We are primarily focusing on someone who has consumer debt or student loan debt and not that of utilizing other people's money for investments.

The rich rules over the poor, and the borrower is the slave of the lender.
Proverbs 22:7 ESV

*Owe no one anything, except to love each other, for the one who loves
another has fulfilled the law.*
Romans 13:8 ESV

*The wicked borrows but does not pay back, but the righteous is gener-
ous and gives;*
Psalm 37:21 ESV

*Pay to all what is owed to them: taxes to whom taxes are owed, rev-
enue to whom revenue is owed, respect to whom respect is owed, honor
to whom honor is owed.*
Romans 13:7 ESV

A debtor is a slave to the lender. You cannot solely be a
slave to Christ if you have physical debtors you're constantly
answering to. When I didn't care to properly handle money, I
had tens of thousands of dollars worth of debt. After getting
saved, God spoke to me directly about it through these scriptures. When I tried to pay the money back without investing
time to learn about the laws of money, I failed over and over
again.

In order for me to obey God and pay off my debts, I actually had to think, learn about and manage my money well.
When a person is in debt, you go to work not because it's your
calling but because you have those bills hanging over your
head.

MONEY MATTERS… IF YOU WANT GOD TO TRUST YOU WITH MORE OF IT

*If then you have not been faithful in the unrighteous wealth, who will
entrust to you the true riches?*
Luke 16:11 ESV

Let me share a funny story.

Many years ago when I hadn't learned many of the lessons I will share in this book, I felt the Holy Spirit ask me a question completely out of the blue. He said, "What will you do with surplus?" I had not been thinking about money at all, and because of how it blindsided me, I knew it was Him. I was excited! I knew that if God is asking me what I would do with "surplus", it was because He was planning on entrusting me with it, or so I thought. I took the question seriously and wrote down a list of what I would do with any excess money He gave me on a percentage basis.

I was so confident of how godly this list was and I know that a majority of Christians would look at the list and approve of my heart to give to the kingdom. Based on my knowledge now, I look back on my allocation percentages and I was completely *off base!* I had apportioned every single dollar into giving to one ministry or another. This meant that if God had given me surplus based on my financial knowledge at that time, I would have spent 100% of it within a week and been praying for another miracle of "surplus" in order for us to continue the ministry work we were doing the next year.

When I look back on that list, I laugh so hard because I know that that is *exactly* why God *could not* entrust me with a surplus in that season. In all honesty, I am glad He spared me from it. I already regretted how much I misused what He had previously given to me. I was glad He did not give me more as this would have simply increased that regret.

Parable Of The Talents

In Matthew 25:14-30, Jesus told a parable where a master gave his servants charge of his goods in the form of "talents" while he traveled to a far country. While we often teach about the talents relating to the gifts and abilities God has given us, remember that in this time, talents referred to a large amount of *money*. When the master returned, he assessed how his servants stewarded the money he had left to them. He evaluated them according to how faithful each one was in making wise investments with his talents to gain a profit.

The master expected every one of them to have some profit depending on how much they had been given. This multiplication was equated with that servant being "faithful" while simply returning what was given at face value was deemed "wicked" and "lazy". Jesus' words, not mine.

The master then rewarded his servants according to how each had handled what he had been entrusted with. The two who were found faithful were given more, while the unfaithful servant had the little he had been given, taken away.

Being honest, many of us cannot even say that we could present back to God any face value to demonstrate what we have already been blessed with - much less a profit.

We are praying to be extravagant givers in the kingdom, but if we do not care enough to learn the laws of money, why should God entrust it to us? He is not a gambler! He is not pulling the slot machine crossing his fingers that we get it right this time. He gives us just enough to see what we will do with it and until we are ready for more, He will not give us the more, to spare us.

LET'S GET THE MONEY CONVERSATION STARTED

In short, I believe that we as the body of Christ have not been fair to one another. We expect people to thrive enough financially to give magnanimously, but don't allow each other to have the necessary conversations about money to help us get there. We can do better. So, let's put on our big boy and big girl pants and recognize that money is a topic that matters in the 21st century. If we want to maximize our impact for good, we must face and conquer it head on!

Below I have included an excerpt from a speech "Acres of Diamonds" Russell Conwell gave across America in the 1800s. He was a Baptist pastor, an orator, philanthropist, lawyer, and writer. He was also the founder of Temple University in Philadelphia.

"I say that you ought to get rich, and it is your duty to get rich. How many of my pious brethren say to me, "Do you, a Christian minister, spend your time going up and down the country advising young people to get rich, to get money?" "Yes, of course I do." They say, "Isn't that awful! Why don't you preach the gospel instead of preaching about man's making money?" "Because to make money honestly is to preach the gospel." That is the reason. The men who get rich may be the most honest men you find in the community.

"Oh," but says some young man here to-night, "I have been told all my life that if a person has money he is very dishonest and dishonorable and mean and contemptible." My friend, that is the reason why you have none, because you have that idea of people. The foundation of your faith is altogether false. Let me say here clearly, and say it briefly, though subject to discussion which I have not time for here, ninety-eight out of one hundred of the rich men of America are honest. That is why they are rich. That is why they are trusted with money. That is why they carry on great enterprises and find plenty of people to work with them. It is because they are honest men.

Says another young man, "I hear sometimes of men that get millions of dollars dishonestly." Yes, of course you do, and so do I. But they are so rare a thing in fact that the newspapers talk about them all the time as a matter of news until you get the idea that all the other rich men got rich dishonestly.

My friend, you take and drive me—if you furnish the auto—out into the suburbs of Philadelphia, and introduce me to the people who own their homes around this great city, those beautiful homes with gardens and flowers, those magnificent homes so lovely in their art, and I will introduce you to the very best people in character as well as in enterprise in our city, and you know I will. A man is not really a true man until he owns his own home, and they that own their homes are made more honorable and honest and pure, and true and economical and careful, by owning the home.

For a man to have money, even in large sums, is not an inconsistent thing. We preach against covetousness, and you know we do, in the pulpit, and oftentimes preach against it so long and use the terms about "filthy lucre" so extremely that Christians get the idea that when we stand in the pulpit we believe it is wicked for any man to have money—until the collection-basket goes around, and then we almost swear at the people because they don't give more money. Oh, the inconsistency of such doctrines as that!

Money is power, and you ought to be reasonably ambitious to have it. You ought because you can do more good with it than you could without it. Money printed your Bible, money builds your churches, money sends your missionaries, and money pays your preachers, and you would not have many of them, either, if you did not pay them. I am always willing that my church should raise my salary, because the church that pays the largest salary always raises it the easiest. You never knew an exception to it in your life. The man who gets the largest salary can do the most good with the power that is furnished to him. Of course he can if his spirit be right to use it for what it is given to him.

I say, then, you ought to have money. If you can honestly attain unto riches in Philadelphia, it is your Christian and godly duty to do so. It is an awful mistake of these pious people to think you must be awfully poor in order to be pious.

Some men say, "Don't you sympathize with the poor people?" Of course I do, or else I would not have been lecturing these years...

A gentleman gets up back there, and says, "Don't you think there are some things in this world that are better than money?" Of course I do, but I am talking about money now. Of course there are some things higher than money. Oh yes, I know by the grave that has left me standing alone that there are some things in this world that are higher and sweeter and purer than money. Well do I know there are some things higher and grander than gold. Love is the grandest thing on God's earth, but fortunate the lover who has plenty of money. Money is power, money is force, money will do good as well as harm. In the hands of good men and women it could accomplish, and it has accomplished, good.

I hate to leave that behind me. I heard a man get up in a prayer-meeting in our city and thank the Lord he was "one of God's poor." Well, I wonder what his wife thinks about that? She earns all the money that comes into that house, and he smokes a part of that on the veranda. I don't want to see any more of the Lord's poor of that kind, and I don't believe the Lord does. And yet there are some people who think in order to be pious you must be awfully poor and awfully dirty. That does not follow at all. While we sympathize with the poor, let us not teach a doctrine like that.[2]

ACTIVATION POINT:

- Get real with yourself. In what ways have you been in denial about the importance of getting money right in your life?
- What has this affected around you? Your family? Relationships? Marriage? Calling and destiny?
- Make a commitment to learn and change as is necessary to honour God in your finances as well as in every other area of your life.

References:
1. Derek Schneider, Beyond The Four Walls (History Makers Publishing, 2014), 36-37.
2. Russell H. Conwell, Acres of Diamonds (New York: Harper Brothers, 1915), 17–22.

CHAPTER 3

Change Your Mind.
Change Your Life.

Before freedom comes a knowing, a belief.

— Toyin Crandell

---

*I urge you therefore, brothers, by the mercies of God, to offer your
bodies as a living sacrifice, holy and pleasing to God, your spiritual worship. Do not conform yourselves to this age but be* **transformed by the renewal of your mind**, *that you may discern
what is the will of God, what is good and pleasing and perfect.*
Romans 12:1-2
*That you should put away the old self of your former way of life,
corrupted through deceitful desires, and be* **renewed in the spirit
of your minds**, *and put on the new self, created in God's way in
righteousness and holiness of truth.*
Ephesians 4:22-24

*"...And you will **know** the truth, and the truth will set you free."*
John 8:32 ESV

Before freedom comes a knowing, a belief.

Limiting Beliefs Can Be Deadly

My business was marketed primarily to women for the first few years, even though we've had a few men join along the way.

Why was that?

About 4 years ago, I ran a Christian ministry which had men and women working together. We had more men than women which wasn't the norm around us. During that time, a man had a long argument with me - more like an impassioned monologue - about how wrong it was for me, as a woman, to direct a ministry that had men under my leadership.

Looking back, I realized that after that *one* conversation, I phased the men out of the ministry in both leadership and then as participants. I focused only on working with, growing and discipling women. After transitioning from evangelistic ministry to my business, I was not actively interested in teaching men. I believed that I was disqualified from leading men simply because I was a woman.

It's interesting because I never verbally assented to that person's statements because I knew of specific female leaders in scripture like warrior Deborah, Queen Esther, Miriam, Apostle Junia, Deacon Pheobe, Priscilla, etc. I didn't even realize it had sunk in because I so firmly disagreed with him at the time, but the seed had been planted.

I was running a finance *business* that didn't accept men. That's like having a bank and turning a guy away solely because the CEO is female. I had over a dozen men ask, "Toyin, can you please run a program that I can participate in?"

"Toyin, I'm the sole breadwinner for my home and we're struggling. Do you teach men?"

I even had a conversation with a man who, while deciding to work with us, said, "I don't care what colour your hair is, whether you're a guy or woman, you have the answer I've been praying for!"

He didn't know that I was just getting over that myself.

Can you believe that I had been isolating 50% of the people who were actively asking for my service because of one tiny conversation I had many many years before?

That is the power of one mindset roadblock!

When this realization hit me during one of my personal retreats, I thought, "Wow, this is exactly the type of thinking that limits so many people and they die without ever knowing it. They think they are making their decisions based on the circumstances around them, their choice, what works, etc. just like I had justified my focus on women on the fact that I really understood their language."

In the retreat, I remembered a 65-year-old client who had struggled financially all her life because of what an authority figure told her when she was 12 years old. When she completed the first part of _Money Mindset SHIFT._, focused on identifying her roadblocks and taking them out from the root, she said, "I can't believe I've lived under that lie for the last 53 years. I didn't even realize my mind was still shaped by that sentence!"

Another client in his early 60s identified a season in his life that affected him for over 30 years. He and his wife were manipulated and cheated financially, which triggered negative feelings related to money. This meant that both of them -

without realizing it - would get rid of any bit of money that touched their hands as soon as possible.

They didn't want money around them because it had disappointed them before. Money meant trouble, they didn't want trouble, and so they didn't want money. They worked ridiculously hard, earned hundreds of thousands over their lifetime and had nothing to show for it because subconsciously, they didn't want to have any.

This led to bad financial decisions and a serious state of lack in a season of their lives when they should have been winding down on work and easing into retirement. Thankfully this is not the end of their story.

I'M HERE ON A "MISSION"

Limiting beliefs, like being "on a mission" are what cause perfectly capable and brilliant workers to stay in a job where they are undervalued and underpaid for years. I remember a client who was being grossly underpaid. Right from our first session, I pointed this out to her. You are working for less than minimum wage, *on purpose!* She said she felt the "Holy Spirit" had her there on a mission to serve that company and influence the atmosphere. I didn't argue with her. We simply began our exercise of discovering what roadblocks were lurking behind the surface. I wasn't surprised when she discovered that she had a deeply rooted lack of awareness of her worth and value.

In this position, she was not able to live her life at all. She was constantly stressed, worried about bills being paid and worried about her retirement. By the time we exposed that root, she realized that the voice telling her to stay was not the Holy Spirit, but the feeling that this is what she "deserved". After digging out that root and realizing her workplace value, *three days later* she received a $12,000 raise in the *same* position with the *same* company from a short 30-minute conversation with her boss. That my friends, is the power of your mind and I could tell you story after story.

The scariest part of limiting beliefs for many Christians is that we think our fear/shame/guilt is the voice of God but it is not. It's fear. It's a commitment to poverty because that's all you may think is possible for you. It's the part of your mind that finds comfort in the familiarity of debt.

In the word of God, there is no place where God tells us to be indebted financially to others. If He wants us to be debt free, why would He counsel us to be paid less than we're worth, have bills that exceed our expenses and give no guidance on how to become and stay debt free? God is a good Father and He is not setting you up to fail.

YOU MUST CHANGE HOW YOU THINK

Many people want to simply affirm their way out of financial struggle without addressing the mental blueprints and thinking patterns that led them there in the first place.

But like Kris Vallotton, a pastor in Bethel Church, Redding said once, *"You don't produce what you want to produce. You reproduce what you see at the watering hole (mirror) of your imagination."*

"Watch your thoughts, they become words;
watch your words, they become actions;
watch your actions, they become habits;
watch your habits, they become character;
watch your character, for it becomes your destiny."
Anonymous.

Death and life are in the power of the tongue,

And those who love it will eat its fruit.

Proverbs 18:21

Before something is spoken outwardly, it started in the mind. Therefore death and life start with the thoughts you harbour in your mind.

As a man thinks in his heart so is he.

Proverbs 23:7

Everything begins in your mind. Whether good or bad. Murder begins as anger that goes unregulated in the mind. A marriage affair never starts with that spouse jumping into bed with someone else (Matthew 5:28). It started when they stopped being mindful to pay attention and care for their own marriage. It started in the mind. In the same way, financial struggle or success will first begin, in your mind.

Do A Self-Evaluation

You must be willing to be honest about where you are in life. You need to get real with yourself about the negative financial patterns you have been putting up with for months or years. This type of self-evaluation isn't done to beat yourself up, feel ashamed, condemned or limited by these weaknesses. It is done because you cannot *fix* what you don't *see!*

You need to realize the areas of your life that, if improved, will allow you to obey God more freely while improving your family's quality of life, career, ministry, finances and even your relationship with God. No one, outside of Jesus Christ Himself, can say they have mastered life and are currently in a place of complete perfection in character, knowledge, wisdom and the like. Everyone has blind spots and limiting beliefs, to pretend you don't is foolish.

Unfortunately, I know of people who expect to become a better reflection of God on the earth without effort on their part. They expect that *God* is changing them and will continue to "work on them" outside of their input. I have actually heard some people say, "God's still working on me" as a cop out from accepting their bad character. That phrase can be used as truth only when you're actively participating with God on that work. Otherwise, you should be saying, **"God wants to work on me but my pride, love for sin and/or stubbornness refuses to allow Him to do His thing"**.
Selah.

Then "who am I" you ask? The person you are right now before you engage in this task of digging out the junk, is a reflection of your parents, family, peers, education, religious upbringing or lack thereof and environment. You have not yet begun to discover who God created you to be unless you have decided to begin self-evaluation. You've simply taken on the expectations of people around you and lived the life they've expected or not expected for the most part.

Like it or not, you are the subtotal of your circumstance, and those who developed and trained you. Those who contributed to your upbringing have helped establish your present mindset and paradigm for life and finance. Even if everything looks good, and you have done well in this role, without self-evaluation and improvement, you have not yet started living your own life. You are living the one they created for you.

My Sisters and I

Let's take a brief look at how our environments affected my siblings and I. Though I have four sisters, three of us, including myself spent most of our childhood in Nigeria. The last 2 were raised, by the same parents in Canada. This affected our way of thinking and behaviour drastically.

For example, in Nigeria, for our family, expressing love through touch wasn't a huge focus. We knew our parents loved us. They worked hard to provide for us, gave us really wonderful travel experiences and spent a lot of time sitting with and teaching us. At the end of each day, we normally prayed together as a family then my sisters and I, the oldest three, said goodnight to our parents and went to bed.

After moving to Canada, I will never forget the day we had prayer time and once we finished, our youngest sister went up to daddy for a hug, a kiss and asked him to read her a bedtime story. I remember thinking, "Wow! That has never happened before!" It soon became a norm for them and eventually expressing love through hugs and touch became a norm for all of us. Thank God for parents who are willing to learn and adapt to what is good.

Some things that come naturally to the three of us raised mostly in Nigeria, are an afterthought for my 2 sisters raised in Canada. On the other hand, there are parts of Canadian culture that are very much a part of them and had to be learned for the three of us.

I remember this one instance almost 15 years ago in particular. It was the first time we ever went to a camp in Canada. We spent a full week immersed in Canadian culture. After getting home and telling all the exciting stories to our parents, my dad asked one of my sisters to wash the dishes.

She said no.

We were all shocked. In Nigeria, we were taught never to disrespect authority and to obey our parents. Saying no would *not* have been a thought much less a response for those of us who were raised in Nigeria. Long story short, she washed those dishes.

We are vastly different simply because of one change in our upbringing, our environment. Likewise, there are paradigms through which you look at life that cannot be shared or given. And these paradigms can limit or affect who you become and your ability to complete the task God has placed you on this planet for, if you are not committed to a process of self-evaluation and eventually, change.

This is not meant to be proud self-discovery to inspire self-worship, but a prayerful look at God's desire for who you are supposed to be and a commitment to live the life you are meant to live for His glory.

You CAN Change How You Think!

God is amazing! I mean that. He is wise, extraordinary, creative, excellent and is completely outside of our scope of understanding. I remember watching a video called the "Inner Life of the Cell" during my University biology days. I was awestruck by the precision, intricacy and wonderful creativity that works inside of one cell. This led me to think about how many different cells work together to help our organs function and how our organs work together to enable us to live.

I was a student of science and I was in awe. Imagine my surprise when my professor ended the video by saying, "Look at how messy that all was. If there was a God, why would He make it so messy?" and I thought, "Prof, that mess is what enables you to think that thought and speak it to us coherently." Since I've started to study the human mind and brain in the field of Neuroscience, I have fallen in love with the wisdom and beauty of God in His creation all over again.

This isn't just me geeking out on the science of the mind. It is because I can now see both the power He has placed in our mind to function as well as the ability He has given to *every single human being* to change their way of thinking and thereby change their life experience. I will give you an example of when I started to notice this ability.

My Former Boss' Salads

In one of my earlier workplaces, one of my boss' would eat so healthy, I honestly thought she was punishing herself (only slightly joking). She would eat huge salads for lunch, fish as a snack and fruits and vegetables when she was randomly hungry. The only time I ever saw her order a pizza, I remember it loaded up with all sorts of vegetables and anchovies. It definitely was not your normal pizza at all, *at least not mine.*

I had to know if she actually enjoyed all these vegetables she was constantly eating. "Don't you wish you were having burgers, or chips for lunch or snacks sometimes," I asked. To which she responded, "No, I really enjoy it. I love the taste, and if I don't have my salads or nuts I miss it." This shocked me. I understood eating healthy only as a means of being healthy, not enjoyment. I did not understand taste buds actually preferring it to a good steak or some rice and stew.

So I continued to ask, "How did you get this way? Were you always like this?" She responded, "No. When I was 21 years old, I ate like the average Canadian. Junk food regularly and didn't really pay attention to what I was putting in my body. Then one day I decided that eating healthy was important to me, so I began to train my tastebuds to enjoy healthy foods. I simply started eating healthy and now I've stuck to it for a long, long time."

A few decades later, her taste buds have now adapted to her inner value system. The love for healthy living and clean eating.

My Own Health Journey

At that time I didn't think I needed to eat or live healthily.

I had been pretty slim most of my life and never cared about it at all. I was a meatatarian, pasta, and rice loving overeater. Fast forward a full year after I had my first daughter. My habits began to show their fruit and I was still carrying the baby weight. This was not what I had expected. Back in the day, I could eat whatever I wanted, do a minimal amount of physical activity, fast every now and then and I'd be back in "shape". I tried over and over to lose the baby weight but it wasn't going anywhere. This was during the time I started asking God to change how I thought.

I read a book called *Healthy and Fit* by Beni Johnson and in it, she simply addressed the possibility of fitness for everyone, even extreme *non*-fitness fanatics like myself. As I journaled about what she was teaching, I began to ask myself various questions regarding my beliefs around health and weight. I realized that I believed two serious lies that were limiting my ability to lose weight and live an overall healthy life.

It was extremely silly but I'll tell you.

I believed that "black women put on weight as they aged" and "all this fitness and clean eating is a white girl thing."

Because I believed that subconsciously, I figured this weight I had put on from having my first child was just the beginning of a life of being overweight. Because this was so deeply rrooted and subconscious, I had never truly tried to change. I gave up or sabotaged my health journey so even when I took the right actions, it wouldn't work.

I then asked myself another question: Is this true? I realized that while I had only focused on the black women who had put on weight as they aged or who ate like me at that time, there are *many* examples of other black women who were healthy and fit well into their 80s! I realized that while I was inundated by social media with pictures of fit white women who were all health coaches, there were also tons of black women who were making great health decisions, choosing to live fit lives and coaching as well.

I realized how silly both beliefs were. Now that I noticed and addressed both of them I was able to *shift* my way of thinking. Within 3 months I had lost all the baby weight, was eating healthier than I had ever eaten in my life, found joy in it, and was on top of my health game.

I remember one night my husband, daughter and I had mixed vegetables and fish for dinner. I said to him, "Babe I'm stuffed." He responded, "Toyin, do you remember when food wasn't food unless there was rice or pasta included? Or how you used to eat 2 to 3 plates before you were done? You're full on one serving of veggies and fish! Who are you?" We almost rolled on the floor laughing, but that's literally how much I had changed.

The change happening internally enabled me to maintain this new way of living without exerting as much effort once I started. This is one of the reasons so many people who start diets without shifting their mindsets revert back to old habits once the diet pressure is gone.

Learning Marketing

Another way I realized how possible it was to change quickly and permanently was in the area of marketing. For many years as I ran the not for profit ministry, marketing was one of our biggest challenges. It culminated in 2015, we published 2 books, released 4 albums, choreographed and organized an international flash mob with the Pan Am Games (a major sporting event in the Americas) and much more in the space of 12 months. At the end of the year, we had an Art Showcase where we blended media, dance, step, music, visual art, spoken word and much more in one event. It was an extraordinary 3-hour show that we had worked on all year.

The photographer came up to us at the end of the show and said, "I have never seen anything like I witnessed here tonight. Why were there only 50 people here to see this? It was FREE! Why did you not market it more?" I told him that marketing had been our challenge for years and we had been praying for God to send us someone who could take on the marketing for our products and programs.

Guys, I can show you leadership team agendas and minutes for 3 years straight with this prayer point on it, "God send us a marketing person!" The photographer told me, "Well I can't do it for you guys, but I can teach you the basics of social media marketing in a couple of sessions if you'd like." We agreed and presented the opportunity to everyone in our organization. Only 3 of us (myself, my husband and Mia Thomas) took advantage of the training but by the end of it, we knew the basics for Youtube and a bit more about Instagram and Facebook.

I was starting from ground zero. For years, I had been proudly disconnected and social media illiterate because I figured using social media to promote ministry work was for people who wanted to "build their own name" but I'm here to build Christ's name. Unfortunately, no one could hear the message of Christ we had to share because of that false humility.

So we took ownership of our marketing. We decided that if God wasn't going to send us a marketer, we could create our own social media plans and execute them.

We had an annual summer outreach mission program, where most of the participants were from our warm network and we usually received about 5 applications from outside of that. After understanding the impact, message and opportunity to serve more people through marketing, we received 29 applications to participate.

Because I had taken the time to learn the language of our generation - social media - the message God had given me to share began to reach the people who were praying to hear it. Three years later my husband runs a full *social media marketing* company while I teach people how to use social media to market their businesses. I receive hundreds of leads each month through social media and understand it like it's a native language.

I never thought this was possible for me. I used to think that all online webinars were really live. I did not understand the concept of automated emails. But once I decided that this information was necessary for where God was calling me, I studied it and it's now easy as pie.

I knew about God, the Bible and how to apply His word but almost nothing about specific practical business needa. I can tell story after story of my decision to teach myself whatever was necessary in order to enhance my ability to do what He's called me to do.

LOVING GOD WITH ALL YOUR MIND

"Teacher, which is the great commandment in the Law?" And He said to him, "'You shall love the Lord your God with all your heart, and with all your soul, and with all your mind.'
Matthew 22:36,37

I love this scripture. It is the foundation of my entire life. I am also a very passionate person, so when I think about expressing my love for God I go all out. It's easy for us to love God with our words. It's more difficult to love Him with our actions through focused obedience. I truly believe it is the hardest of all but the most wonderful of all, to love Him with our mind.

He wants this for us! He has given us the mind of Christ, but so many of us refuse to renew our minds so that we actually live and experience, "Christ in us, the hope of glory!" So we continue living with the junk of our former selves. We settle for our B.C. (before Christ) minds and pray for God to come down to earth and change our external circumstances almost magically.

It's like being on autopilot and living your life based on what you saw and experienced growing up. We have left the destiny God has given to each of us to chance when He has given us an ability to hear where He has called us to, change our mind and shift course as needed. If He called us to love Him with all our *mind* it is because He knew it was possible. We can change our mindset to bring it into greater alignment with His way of thinking.

His thoughts will always be much much higher than our thoughts but He invites us to meet with Him and learn from Him. He invites us to be open-minded in hearing His voice and believing the truth that is in His written word.

What Is Your Value System Based On, Culture Or God?

I remember the day I encountered one of the errors in my culture and had to choose what held more value for me. I had gotten into an argument with my younger sister. Afterward, in my time of prayer, I felt the Holy Spirit tell me to return to her and apologize for the way I had spoken to her.

For context: I grew up in the Nigerian culture which says the older person is always right. And I genuinely **believed** that. I would always take the word of an elder person over someone younger. Therefore, I would also assume that I was in the right if I disagreed with someone younger than me.

When Abba asked me to humble myself by apologizing to my younger sister, I immediately protested. I said, "I can't do that, she's younger than me!" I thought that, even if I was wrong in the way I spoke to her, she was wrong for arguing with me in the first place. She wasn't being respectful towards me. As I wrestled with this request, I thought, "I can't apologize to her, that just doesn't make sense." To which He said, "You are either first a Nigerian or you are first My follower. Which is it?"

Immediately, I conceded that before I could lay claim on any other part of my identity, I needed to submit my entire person, identity and *way of thinking* to God and His word before my nationality or culture. In particular, I had to submit my pride, though it was acceptable culturally. For the sake of having a relationship with my sister that reflected the love of Christ, I apologized to my sister. I mumbled a pathetic "sorry" which was really surprising to her and quenched much of our fire, for that moment.

This didn't make me less of a Nigerian, or less connected to my culture. However, it helped me to look objectively at what parts of my culture and its influence on my way of thinking were aligned with the word of God and what parts were not.

That simple action shifted my paradigm.

My changed mind on this issue proved very helpful during our premarital marriage counselling. An elder person counselled myself and my husband, then-fiance by saying that we needed to plan financially (good advice) and that in order to do that well, we needed to love money. Bad advice. Really *really* bad advice.

I thought I misheard him the first time, but he kept on repeating that *loving* money was good and it was such a glaring opposite from the word of God. If I still had that mindset of elders and those in authority always being right, I may not have caught on to what he was saying at all.

Now, in my Canadian culture, there is an emphasis on being non-confrontational and not stirring the pot. If fitting into my Canadian culture was more important to me than obedience to God, this book would not be in your hands. I would have learned everything I needed to learn, continued running my business and kept silent about all of this, in order not to offend anyone.

When other inconsistencies between my culture (Canadian or Nigerian) and the Word of God presented themselves, I was much more likely to notice it and choose God's word and His way.

So, you need to know what your current value system and mindset about money is based on. Is it the amalgamation of everyone else's opinion and traditions or is it founded on the Word of God? Here's the deal. You have greater potential for growth and change than you can ever imagine. You are able to determine what your values are for life and change your lifestyle, paradigms, habits, and mode of thinking to live a life that follows those values. You can recreate your life experience by changing your way of thinking and habits to match the principles that are most important to you.

ACTIVATION POINT

Ask yourself these questions:
- Have I been on autopilot for a month? A year? A few years? Decades?
- Have I ever assessed my own thoughts and beliefs to see whether it has been helping or sabotaging my progress in life and specifically in my finances?
- Have I identified what type of beliefs I've been carry-

ing for years that have allowed me to produce a fair level of success but "never quite there"?

- Make a list of the different modes of thought that you have, which have been inspired by your upbringing, culture, education, peers, etc.

- Highlight any of them that you can see clearly are not reflective of the word of God or your vision for your own life.

- List out the values or qualities you see in people you admire or are doing work in the sphere you are called to. You do not have to "be" them. In fact, you can't but you can learn from them. What qualities have contributed to their success?

- If you have been called to serve homeless and orphaned children, you want to seek out the qualities in people like Mother Teresa, Heidi Baker, etc. that have helped them impact those children. You may not have the same level of influence that they do, but that's not the point. It's about affecting the children you are called to, period.

- If you value having a strong united family while achieving specific goals in your career, what are the qualities you see in strong united families with parents and spouses who are making strides in their careers around you?

- If you can't find any of these types of families in your immediate circle of friends, read books and do an online search to find examples.

It's time to wake up! It's time to make it a priority to take your mind back and bring it under submission to Christ in all areas of your life.

CHAPTER 4

Stop Doing What's Not Working

If you head east looking for the sunset,
you've got a problem!

— Doren Aldana

Now let's get practical. The first thing you will need to do in order to change your financial situation is to take a step back from the rat race, your general busyness and **reflect**.

Take the time to specifically identify anything you've been doing that is not working. Whether that is refinancing your home, filing for bankruptcy, trying to get additional qualifications, simply working "harder", committing and recommitting to a budget, saying positive affirmations and faith declarations, or any other gimmick that you are learning from Youtube and Google.

You need to be willing to pause and think to yourself, "Has my financial situation changed positively and permanently with all of this?"

Reflect on the last few months, then the last few years. Are there any repetitive, negative financial patterns in cycles of months, or years? Write them down.

DEBT CONSOLIDATION, HOME REFINANCING, BANKRUPTCY

For example, have you ever used debt consolidation, home refinancing or bankruptcy to clear your debts? Or have you ever paid off all your debts in the past? If you succeeded but created another debt load after 2, 5 or 10 years, this is a clear symptom that the problem is not in clearing your debt. There is a deeper problem behind this reoccurring financial crisis that must be addressed.

While writing this book, I spoke with two families who shared the most frustrating bank stories. One woman, visited her bank to find out the exact amount she would need to pay monthly to pay off her debts and get above the interest cycle. The bank employee told her the best thing to do would be to roll all her debt into her mortgage. She already had a ballooned mortgage because this is what *another* bank employee told her to do last year.

The year before, she trusted their advice, went ahead and put her debt into her mortgage. In the next 12 months, she incurred even more additional debts because she hadn't changed.

A few days later, I spoke to a couple who had been given similar advice. They were told by the bank that the way to "fix" their debt issue was to once again, "roll it into their mortgage". So they did that. Twice. And now? They have a ballooned mortgage *plus* new debt that was stifling them. By the time they contacted our team, they were under triple the stress they had before taking that advice because once again, *they* hadn't changed.

People don't seem to notice that the bank's *profit* is in your interest payments! It's like going to an undertaker and asking him how to live a longer life; his work begins after you die! No offense to any undertakers reading. What am I trying to say? It's easy to consolidate, file for bankruptcy, refinance the house to cover the debt. These options work for some. But a majority of those who do it are left worse than they began. Like John Maxwell, an author, speaker, and pastor who has written many books focused on leadership says "There are no shortcuts to any place worth going."

These two families were so sick and tired of their situation. They heard about what we've been able to help others do - pay off debt, break overspending habits, plan their finances and watch the plan work. They got on the phone with us, committed to their permanent change and now have a clear game plan for their debt freedom.

Not only that, they have brought in more income to help them get there faster. They have changed their habits and because of that, have actually paid off debt, something they had been desperately trying to do for years.

You can do it too.

No more words.

No more complaining.

No more stress.

BUDGETS, BUDGETS, AND MORE BUDGETS

Everyone and their mama has heard experts say if you want to be financially free, you need to use a budget. It's a good concept. In fact, I love budgets so much that I use a monthly spending plan, and I teach people how to create strong monthly spending plans.

However, from my conversations with thousands of people stuck in bad financial patterns, simply creating a budget does not change their picture. Why? It's easy to jump from budget to budget. Excel documents, mobile apps, banking technology make it easy to fool yourself into thinking that you are making progress financially because you've mastered the latest budgeting system.

These things may give you the motivation to track your spending and pull things together for a few months, but not long-term. The budget becomes a tracking tool that is simply telling you that you are in the red each month. That's not the purpose of the budget.

Just because you are *tracking* your spending, doesn't mean you are *changing* your spending.

Just because you are using a budget, doesn't mean you actually know *where* to put the money when you have a savings goal or debt freedom goal.

It's time to look at your behaviour. How many times have you started a new budget and stopped? How much has a budget actually changed your financial reality?

Some people created a budget, got it working smoothly for them and turned everything around. So what is the main difference? Those who have turned things around have done the internal work, dealing with the core issues needed to become financially free. This allows them to stick to a good budget and get it working for them without sabotaging themselves. If this foundational work is not done, the budget is nothing but fancy tech or a piece of paper.

WORKING HARDER IS NOT THE ANSWER

"Just work harder." This is a classic response from many experts to people who are struggling financially. One of the challenges with this is that often, people who are struggling are actually working physically harder than others. They are putting in 40-70 hour weeks, plus overtime, working 2-3 jobs but find themselves earning less than they're worth and have nothing to show for it at the end of the month.

Many people are hustling like there's no tomorrow, and just barely getting by. They are working so much they miss out on being with family, enjoying life and those around you would say that this is normal.

"You work and work and get nothing for it." Or they'll say, "Making money is hard for everyone. It's just the way things are in order to take care of your family or your future."

That's all *bogus*. Many of you have parents who have worked extremely hard all of their lives. I want you to ask yourself, "Has all of the hard work they've done in their lifetime made them financially free?" For as long as you actually believe hard work or more qualifications alone will lead you to become financially wealthy or free, you may never get there, because it's impossible to work physically hard enough to earn substantial wealth.

You can work hard enough to just get by, but how many hours can you actually work to have an extra $5,000 in income each month? How much harder can you actually work to have that money working for you in life? Many people are literally on the fast track to burning out attempting this strategy if they're not already there.

Here's what I know for a fact: until you are willing to stop playing the "just work harder" game, until you get really sick and tired of doing what every other normal, overworked and still financially stuck person is doing, you will, unfortunately, continue to struggle financially. Until you're ready to address the root issues that have been holding back your favor and flow in finances and in life, you're not yet ready for financial freedom.

All the people who are telling you, "You can't work less and earn more in your field," say so because they can't. Think about this: Are there are other people in your field who work less than you do but earn more? Are there others with the same and even fewer qualifications who earn more? This isn't about comparison. It's about getting to the facts. Now, what makes you different from them? Your mindset.

Let me show you why I am convinced of this.

Several months ago, we had a woman participate in our *Money Mindset SHIFT.* program. When transitioning into the program, she told me, "Toyin, there isn't any extra money in my company for me, in fact, "people in my profession, my entire field aren't well paid."

She was in the non-profit sector and this was the constant message she'd heard in that environment, including her time at University and throughout her working life. She had already asked for a raise from her manager and was told, "there is no extra money here for you." So when I told her that was not the case, that there was *more* available to her, she needed to see it to believe it.

After just a few weeks of addressing the real issues that were holding her back from moving forward, she was offered a $5,000 raise at that same workplace by the same manager who had told her there was "no extra money", without needing to ask again. They all of a sudden "found money" and were ready to offer it to her. However, she did not immediately take them up on their offer because that same day, she was scheduled for a job interview, for a very similar position that paid $15,000 more than what she was receiving at her present place of work.

A few days later she sent me this message:

"TOYIN!!! I GOT THE JOB!!!! Out of 150 applicants!!!! They chose ME!!!!! … It gets better!!!... They are offering me $22,000 MORE THAN MY CURRENT SALARY."

This was for a different job from what she went in to interview for. A job she *did not apply directly for.* This was without getting any "extra" qualifications or designations. This was without having to add 20 more hours of work to her week. This job came to her because she *finally* got out of her own way and changed her strategy for financial freedom.

Her entire financial goal for that year was completed within ONE MONTH of doing something different from what she had done for years.

IF I CAN JUST EARN MORE, THINGS WILL GET BETTER

So many people believe if they earn more, things will better. However, I have had numerous conversations with people who earn $10,000+/month who are just as "broke" as if they earned $2,000/month.

Several years ago, I spoke with a woman who was stuck in a place of lack. Money was never enough. She didn't understand why she thought like this because she came from a wealthy background. Her father was a medical doctor and earned $300,000 annually. After we did some digging, it turned out that even though he earned $300,000 each year, he spent about $350,000. This caused numerous arguments, an eventual divorce and left his entire family in a state of lack, fear, and anxiety whenever they thought about or handled money.

Some people assume that if they could only earn more, they would be able to invest, do more and hit their financial goals. Think about it, since you've started your career until now, has your pay grade changed? Were you earning less when you got started in your career? Probably. Has that increase in your income led to financial freedom for you today? For some people, probably not. Some say, "If only I could earn more, things will not be so tight." But you're already earning more than you were years ago, and things are still tight. Just "earning more" is not the solution.

CUTTING EXPENSES DOESN'T CUT IT

Have you ever been told that to become debt free and have savings, you'll need to be extremely strict with spending? Were you told that you must deprive yourself of any enjoyment or spending on fun things until you've hit those goals? Let me save you some hard work and aggravation.

Years ago, I tried that exact same strategy. I had not been on a vacation in seven years - *seven years!* I cut eating out. I brought my expenses down to the bare, *bare* bones. I believed that if I could just reduce my expenses as much as possible, *then* I would have the extra cash to get above this place of lack and do the things I knew I needed or wanted to do. But what really happened?

I learned the hard way. Cutting my expenses was only a small part of what was needed for financial freedom. For the first few months, you may feel great about negotiating things like your car insurance, phone bill, and everything else down to the bones. You may even save a few hundred bucks. But, that feeling often doesn't last because it didn't actually change your habits or end the pattern of self-sabotage.

Cutting my expenses didn't teach me how to change my mindset. It didn't teach me to make the money I was bringing in actually work for me instead of dissipating. When I focused solely on reducing expenses, my income literally reduced to match my then lower expenses and things remained just as hard as they had been for years.

It didn't fix our problem of never having enough. It didn't bring us into any level of real financial freedom. I then asked myself a question, "What would happen if I stopped focusing on what else I could cut out and started focusing on changing my mindset and habits? What if I retrained my brain to scale my income so that an extra $50 on a bill is not a source of stress if I needed that service? I shifted my focus from cutting expenses to increasing my income and no longer sabotaging that process. To be honest, by that point there was nothing more left to cut.

I focused on retraining my brain to use that income to benefit my family, church and ongoing short and long-term projects at present and in the future. I decided to give myself permission to enjoy my life and family *now*, not in the distant future. Not after my business became 6 figures. Not after my first million dollars.

I decided to enjoy the journey and within 2 years, we surpassed our income goals. We were able to take the vacations that were barely a dream in the beginning, *and* have savings and investments for our future, without having to sacrifice our sanity or fun during the process.

Am I saying that you shouldn't cut down on your expenses? The truth is, it may help in the beginning but there comes a point where there is just nothing left to cut. I have spoken to hundreds of people who do not a space carved out for fun in their budget. They spend 100% of their money paying bills and trying to survive. They don't have "frills" to cut and stay struggling until they address the full picture.

At some point, you need to fix this from the root and no longer just target the symptoms. You need to be able to scale your income and get money working for and not against you.

POSITIVE AFFIRMATIONS: PUTTING THE CART BEFORE THE HORSE

Some teach others to simply declare and have faith. The truth is, when you simply make faith declarations without finding and uprooting the mindsets that have created your current reality, the cognitive dissonance in your mind reaffirms your present state.

For instance, if a person is currently earning $2,500 a month and has never earned above $4,000 a month, simply telling themselves they earn $6,000 a month without dealing with the real internal doubts that may come up can repeatedly trigger a part of their brain called the Anterior Cingulate Cortex (ACC). The ACC regulates any discrepancies between our beliefs and our actions; so, that person's ACC will remind them that they actually earn $2,500/mth and have never gone above $4000/month.

You can't just muscle through that thought. You have to confront and uproot the limiting beliefs first. Before you can *confront and uproot* the belief, you have to *know* what you believe that is holding you back. That, my friend, will be our focus during Part 2 of this book. Get ready!

You can't solve a problem you don't think you have. Humility is where growth begins.

ARE YOU HEARING ME?

These are just six of many examples I can give of how people continue to target the symptoms and end up right where they started. While this advice is popular, it is only useful when applied in the right way and time. There are only two reasons you're focusing on strategies that are not working for you. One, you haven't taken a step back to look around and see if the strategy is actually working for you. Or two, you keep hearing experts with good intentions tell you to keep doing what all the other financially stuck people are doing.

Why do you need to understand this? If you don't recognize that the issues you've been trying to fix are not the real problem, you will continue to waste your time and efforts trying new budgets, committing and recommitting yourself, scraping to save money, then dipping back into those savings, leaving you right where you got started.

Repeating this cycle for years triggers regret, guilt, frustration, disappointment and eventually causes the person to lose faith in the possibility of changing their financial situation. One woman shared that she had fought and lost for so many years, she was comfortable with her financial lack. She had a debt load of over $90,000 and felt that this was God's will and portion for her life!

The truth is God's will is for His children is to have dominion on this earth, to shine His light so that others can see it and glorify Him. You are not doomed. You are not stuck. If you have been attempting any of these or other things that have not changed your situation, pay very close attention to the coming Chapters, because if applied, they will change your trajectory forever.

ACTIVATION POINT

Do an inventory on which of these or other strategies you have attempted without assessing its effectiveness in your overall picture. Make a decision to deal with the root issues first before applying external strategies.

CHAPTER 5

Discover
Your Money Mindset Roadblocks

The current state of your life, home, relationships and
bank account are a reflection of what you believe.

— Toyin Crandell

Here's the truth, money is neutral. It has no story in itself.
It simply does what it is told and what you think about
it is exactly what you are telling it to do! This powerful truth
can make or break every, single, part of your life.

It isn't about the symptoms you're facing, it's about what
is causing the financially "stuck" cycle you may be experiencing. It is the subconscious thoughts, the broken mindsets and
the wrong perceptions that are keeping you right where you
have been fighting to leave. You are currently living the exact
financial reality you want. Many of you may respond, "No I'm
not Toyin. I am not living the exact financial reality I want. I

want financial freedom, I want savings and the ability to give to the tune of hundreds of thousands to people in need, I want change."

Here's the thing, your logical brain wants these, but your subconscious mind likes this place that you have been stuck at financially for one reason or the other. It likes the comfort of having only just enough.

"Why do you say that Toyin?" It comes back to how your brain has learned to respond over the years. Your brain was created with a desire for safety, comfort, and pleasure, especially your subconscious mind. It is not able to distinguish where the comfort or pleasure is coming from. This is a prime example when discussing substance abuse. This is why someone would choose to do things that are clearly destroying them for temporary pleasure.

We all have core ideas and beliefs that have significantly shaped our emotions and actions that are not our own and not based on reality. People consistently make poor financial decisions because of subconscious, conditioned beliefs about money. You were not born with these limiting beliefs, but because a vast majority of people around you have them, you have been pre-conditioned in a way that is actually detrimental!

When you see repeating negative financial patterns, most often, the root cause is a belief system or internal comfort that you have formed with that routine or situation.

Why would you believe and unconsciously fight for something that holds you back? Why would you even find this comfortable? The reasons are diverse as we all have different histories, upbringing, experiences, influences and create different stories even from the exact same experience. If you don't bridge the gap between the targets your logical mindsets and what your subconscious wants, you will continue to default to your subconscious comfort zone.

Now, as I've mentioned before, the process of discovering what is keeping you stuck in your subconscious may seem scary, but is necessary. You cannot change what you have not identified. A few people have great self-awareness and can recognize some of the beliefs that are holding them back. Unfortunately, many others simply do not see it. You don't know what you don't know!

I will admit that until I spoke to people who earned and managed a higher level of wealth than I did, I didn't even *know* the way I thought and felt about money was off. This was because I was fully immersed in struggle. *For all of us,* seeing things from a different perspective is a first step and necessity in identifying our own personal mindset roadblocks; this is why I created our discovery exercise.

On average, most people who complete our comprehensive discovery exercise to identify their personal money mindset roadblocks, find 30-60 limiting beliefs. Just holding on to one limiting belief is enough to keep a person stuck all their lives. Let's start the discovery process. It's time to uncover some myths that are keeping you stuck.

PART TWO

MYTHS THAT KEEP YOU STUCK

We are about to uncover some of the most common mindsets that I have watched hold thousands of Christians back from the very financial breakthrough they are praying for. There are many more of these mindset roadblocks which affect people from every background. However, here, I will focus in on the top nine that I have found most popular amongst believers.

To further clarify, in the pages to follow, I am speaking to primarily to Christians that have been called to the marketplace, have been functioning lower than their potential and are not seeing the fruit of their labours.

There are other books that can help those of us who have been called to full-time missionary work like The Fully Funded Missionary by Rob Parker.

I am pulling no punches, so buckle your seatbelts and let's get you set free!

MYTH 1

A Lazy Christian's Insurance

"A good man leaves an inheritance to his children's children,
And the wealth of the sinner is stored up for the righteous.

— Proverbs 13:22

A lot of us read the second half of the above verse, "The wealth of the sinner will be given to the righteous" with a mindset that says God will give me other people's hard earned money simply because I'm His child.

WHAT THIS PRODUCES:

This produces Christians who do not do what is necessary to increase their income or build wealth but are waiting for the day they miraculously receive all the wealth that has been stored up for them.

Doing The Prayer Lottery

Just as people 'hope and wish' to gain wealth by flushing their money down the drain on the lottery, many Christians' mindsets are the same. They are playing the lottery for God's blessings and cloaking it as prayer.

"Last year, brother John got a miracle to the tune of $20,000. Two years ago, Kate H. received a miracle of a free house. I will continue to buy my ticket - sorry, I mean, pray and change nothing - until it's my turn for a big miracle like that." — The Lazy Christian

You are more likely to be struck by lightning *four times* over than to win the lottery. The chances of being struck by lightning are one in 10 million, do the math.

You need to bring something of value to others if you expect to be financially rewarded. God will not make money rain on you every month to pay your bills, which is what some of us are low-key praying for. He will not.

Even if you have been called to full-time missionary work, you should be talking with God about *how* He wants to provide for you. If Elijah assumed that the brook would be his way of eating and drinking for the entirety of the drought and famine, he would have died beside that brook (1 Kings 17).

What Is The Truth?

1. You must be adding value to society in order to receive wealth.
2. God doesn't use miracles as a form of sustenance.

YOU HAVE TO LEARN HOW TO ADD VALUE TO SOCIETY.

Before the fall of man, God gave Adam a task to do. He wasn't simply placed in the garden of Eden to enjoy the fruits, chill all day with his wife, Eve and soak in God's presence. God told him to tend the garden and keep it. He had him name all the animals that had been created. See Genesis 2:15. Even after the fall, God maintained His expectation that we would work. And, you better believe that even though we have been redeemed from the curse of unnecessary toiling, He *still* expects us to do work.

What Are You Bringing To The Table?

The fundamental basis for increasing wealth is through exchange or trade. You need to be producing goods or rendering services. You build more wealth by serving more people at a higher level. This is a foundational principle in earning income, like a few of my mentors taught me: "value out = cash in."

What value are you adding? For some people, they add joy to the world and are richly rewarded for it. Walt Disney's goal and stated purpose when he opened up the very first Disneyland was that he has always wanted to *make people happy* through his love for cartoons. He was rewarded for doing that and reinvested his wealth into bringing more and more joy to others. He wasn't simply pursuing money, but following a basic principle of adding value.

You Also Need To Learn How To Properly Use Money.

In Chapter 1, I shared with you my "surplus" story and how God had given me a simple test to see what I had bothered to learn about managing wealth. I failed that test completely. I firmly believe that He did not release any more large amounts of money to me or even have me go into business until I was willing to learn the lessons I needed about how to use and manage it.

I had shown Him that I clearly did not know the laws of money and would have completely wasted it. It was His mercy that kept me!

Believe it or not, it is the same for you. He will not give

you what you cannot bear. Some of you cannot bear wealth with your current habits, patterns and ways of thinking. You will squander it. Or you will hoard it. So you must be committed to learning and applying strong financial principles if you expect to build wealth, not just spouting quick and shallow information that you Googled.

GOD DOESN'T USE MIRACLES AS A FORM OF SUSTENANCE

Many of us want God to provide our daily bread through miraculous actions. I used to be a strong proponent of this type of expectation. I had no concrete plans for changing my financial situation and simply depended on prayer and faith for God to provide my daily needs.

Sure, I saw God work miracles to stop me from starving or being evicted. But, He began to teach me that this is not how He expects me or anyone else of His children to live, especially when we have ample access to opportunities and resources to change. He may have us do this for a season to help us grow in trust, but not all our lives and not if you are called to the marketplace.

Elijah in 1 Kings 17

When God sent Elijah to the brook to be fed by ravens daily, that was a few months in Elijah's years of life. Afterward, He told him to go and be of service to the widow of Zarephath and there, as she received the miraculous provision and healing of God through his faith, he was also fed and sustained.

Manna From Heaven

The children of Israel were fed daily with manna, bread from heaven, for 40 years. Yet, they have existed many years before and after that experience. That was just a snapshot of their history, not the entirety. When they were no longer in the wilderness, He expected them to work the promised land that was flowing with milk and honey if they wanted to eat.

He did not tell them to whistle their way into the land and because they were His children, He would negotiate on their behalf before they arrived. He didn't say those who occupied it before would easily hand the land over to them. He told them they would have to be courageous and do some work. He gave them specific strategies for each war. Some strategies were simple but scary like walking around the walls of Jericho and at other times they had to pick up their swords and fight for their promise.

Yes, God sometimes gives financial miracles when He chooses but that is not the norm. If you keep doing the same thing you've always done, working a basic job and expecting to suddenly become *wealthy*, you will not get there. This is a fact.

You Have Access, Don't Waste It

Most people reading this do not live in a wilderness. In the 21st century, regardless of your country's economy or your personal background, race, lack of or surplus education, if you have access to resources like this book and the internet, it means you have enough access to change things financially. Be willing to humble yourself and learn.

Is Proverbs 13:22 Wrong?

This verse is true when you do things in God's way. You can and will receive from Christians and non-Christians alike *if* you learn how to bring some form of value to the table.

I remember many mentors telling my husband, Joshua and I different variants of this statement: "When you add value to yourself and to the world, money will find you." We were just picking ourselves up out of financial struggle. We didn't believe them. We could simply "add value" to ourselves, read books, learn and change *internally*, insert FULL sarcasm here and we would have more than enough finances for our family after struggling all these years?

We discussed this but didn't take the first mentor seriously until we spoke to another millionaire in a different sector from a different country. He repeated the same things almost word for word, "Add value to yourself and money will find you," and "Value out = cash in." I jokingly said to Josh, "Do they all attend the same (millionaire) school? They're quoting each other." *Finally*, we decided to take them at their word and it turned out to be correct.

SEEK YE FIRST THE KINGDOM OF GOD

> *"But seek first His kingdom and His righteousness, and all these things will be added to you."*
> Matthew 6:33

This is a variation of the earlier verse. I used to read this and assume it meant that if I sought the kingdom of God solely through prayer, fasting, studying the Bible, worship and the like, God would see my desire to know more of Him and pour out the money we needed.

I believed this way until I began to learn what His kingdom looks like. Yes, it does include worship, prayer, fasting, studying the bible but each time Jesus said, "The kingdom of God has come upon you," He was also giving some form of value to his listeners. He was making their lives better through teaching, healing, food, etc.

The Kingdom of God is not just ethereal, it is practical,

tangible and can be encountered today. The kingdom is revealed when you run your business with integrity in the midst of the temptation to cut corners. It is revealed when you honour your clients and give them your best every single time. When you serve your Directors at the office in a focused way and refrain from joining those who gossip and slander you are bringing the Kingdom of God into that workplace and business sector.

When I understood this, "all these things" began to be added to us.

HE WILL GIVE YOU IDEAS

So many of us are waiting on miracles from God while He waits on us to do something. Don't be fooled, God *will not* do your part. God doesn't owe you money. He doesn't owe you anything. He will give you ideas, strength, wisdom, opportunities for providing service or the production of goods to bless and provide for you through it. See Deuteronomy 8:18. You must stop praying for Him to reward laziness, and decide to take whatever actions are necessary.

MYTH 2

Being Poor Is Holy

You shall be holy to me, for I the Lord am holy and have *separated* you from the peoples, that you should be mine.

— Leviticus 20:26

A few years ago, I sent out a survey to over one thousand people who were in debt that had joined my email list because they wanted to be debt-free. In response to one of the questions I asked, an anonymous person said, "Christians are supposed to be poor." I knew immediately, that unless that person changed their belief, they would never get out of poverty much less pay off their debt.

WHAT THIS PRODUCES

This mentality that Christians are meant to be poor or that

being poor is holy produces Christians who need money but are afraid of it. Deep down they prefer the life of financial uncertainty and lack because they feel it makes them a better Christian.

At the same time, they cannot avoid the need to provide for their families and are left internally torn, burnt out and unclear about why all their hard work is producing no change to their finances. They are also unable to support others in poverty or with great need who lack access to the potential opportunities that *they have.*

WHAT'S THE TRUTH?

Not having money does *not* protect a person from loving money, or having it affect their decisions, level of peace or sense of security. Many people assume that because they do not have money, they are free from the love of it. I have met many Christians who do not have money who constantly judge and criticize others simply for having more resources. There are many who let the presence of money or the lack of it consume their minds. For some, they can't help it because things are so stressful for them and they really don't know what to do. It remains a huge source of torment to their hearts and minds. This is a reality for many who live in lack. Mind you, this can *also* be the case for someone with a lot of money who has put his or her trust in it instead of in God.

I remember observing quite a few millionaires at the beginning of my journey and noticing a particular detachment and neutrality toward money. Since then, I have spoken to many who demonstrated what it looks like to be free of the love of it, which is why God could entrust them with it. It reminds me of people in the bible like Job, David, Joseph, Abraham, Isaac who also submitted their money and actions to

God's ultimate will.

Once again, money is simply a tool we can use to do the work of God and meet our needs. Being humble, walking in purity and holiness before God is a matter of the heart and not the numbers in your bank account. The love of money is not a numbers issue, it is a heart issue. No one can judge another person's heart, only God can do that.

What Is Holiness?

The Hebrew word for holy is "qodesh" and means "apartness, set-apartness, separateness, sacredness". God is holy. He is totally above all He has created, including us. In the New Testament, the word for holy is "hagios" and means "set apart, reverend, sacred, and worthy of veneration." This word applies to God because God Himself is totally separate, sacred, transcendent, reverend, and set apart from every created thing.

When God calls us to be holy, He is not calling us to be poor. There are people who are not set apart for the service of God who are poor. He is calling us to be set apart for His service wherever He sends us. If He has called you to work in the marketplace, then giving it all your heart, soul, mind, and strength is what holiness and obedience looks like.

The Victim Mentality

Many Christians who embrace this teaching also embrace a victim mentality: always being beaten and struggling in the practical areas of life as part of the calling of God. A couple once asked us to pray with their family for good jobs for both the husband and wife. They were drowning financially. We prayed together for over a year but nothing was changing. One day, they mentioned that they actually *enjoyed* this place because this was where they could suffer with Christ. I told them there was no point in asking God to change a situation they wanted to keep.

When the Bible speaks to us about picking up our cross and suffering for the sake of the gospel, we aren't to go out looking for suffering. Suffering is not our badge of honour as a Christian. Jesus went through the Garden of Gethsemane, then He went to the cross and guess what? He overcame the world, the grave, death, and sin and gave us His resurrection power.

I have had my share of suffering because life happens and faced persecution here in the West specifically for my belief in Jesus Christ the Messiah. I have suffered without money and suffered with it. I have always faced challenges in pushing to obey God's leadership over my life whether in ministry efforts or business. The more I say yes, the greater the challenges I face. However, I don't pray to suffer so I can prove something to God or those around me. I pray to live my life completely in His will and when challenges come, I lean on Him and expect the resurrection power of God to work in me and bring great good out of it.

The victim mentality has become a cancer in our day and age. Some people love to complain and have those around them feeling sorry for them. People will even base friendships and workplace relationships on wallowing in their suffering: how little they are paid, how unfair their work situation is, how difficult the economy is for their particular business. What a waste!

We talk about God's power to change to those around us and then exempt ourselves from it by believing that He can change everyone else but us. There was an instance where a woman approached me for coaching. She had everything prepared to get started but decided not to do so on her set start date though everything was still in place. She then emailed me saying how sad and stuck she was. She had approached me just so that she could give the same excuse - no one and nothing can help my situation. This was the same victim story she had rehearsed for decades. I responded to her email," You're not stuck. You are making a choice. Own it."

THE OTHER EXTREME

I've also heard others take this to the other extreme and say that if a Christian is struggling financially, they must have sinned or not have enough "faith". I do not believe that one bit. That would be like saying someone who is sick physically is that way because of some sin in their lives or because they do not have faith for healing. See John 9:1-12. It's very easy to try to paint a group of people with the same brush. Sometimes, being stuck in debt or not being financially free could be because that person has not learned how to manage money or how to change decades of negative financial habits.

I loved Jesus fervently and though I was not sinless, I knew that my financial struggles were not because of living a sinful lifestyle. In fact, this was one of the lessons God taught me while I was struggling and not seeing the financial breakthrough I had prayed for. I felt He had given a promise of provision in a specific thing and it didn't happen in the time I expected. I began to search my heart and ask Him what I did wrong to circumvent that promise.

I remembered some of the mistakes I had made in those months of waiting and believing and figured that may have been why I didn't see the fruit. He stepped in quickly and revealed something I will never forget. He said, "Toyin if I withheld My blessings from you because you sinned in these months, you would *never* have access to any blessings from Me because you sin more than you realize!" He also said (paraphrased), "If I loved you enough to adopt you as My daughter when you hated and disregarded Me, why would I love you any less and shun you for your mistakes now that you are My daughter and you are actually fighting to live pure before Me?"

It also wasn't a fault of faith (as you have read). For me, it was a problem with action. For some, it's because they did not have financially savvy parents to tell them what to do with money. There are too many reasons people are stuck financially to provide a cookie-cutter, one size fits all solution.

That is one reason why my coaching practice does not offer a detached online course for everyone to simply run through. They are all assigned a coach who knows their history, current reality, access to resources, mindset and are able to build their way out through an individualized plan. This is why Google and Youtube do not work. Your story and journey is completely different from mine. Sure there are key takeaways from mine and other experts but the most foundational roadblocks in your mind and the plan for rebuilding are a combination that is yours alone.

I Only Want Just Enough

You may have heard conversations insinuating that it is sinful to have more than enough; "You should have just enough for today." *That* type of mentality keeps your subconscious afraid of having the extra needed to save, invest or build wealth. Yet the same Bible says, "A righteous man leaves an inheritance for his children's children" (Proverbs 13:22). What does that mean? It means that you have enough assets not just for your lifetime, not just for your children, but for your grandchildren. That is three generations of wealth! There is a level of investing, saving, building and *instructing* that you will need to do for it to reach your grandchildren.

So if you plan on obeying the word of God by…

- Leaving an inheritance for your children's children…
- Becoming a lender and not a borrower…
- Providing adequately for your household with the rising cost of college tuition, and living expenses...
- Working in a balanced way where you can spend quality time of rest with your family…
- Giving to those in need around you and all over the world…
- Being able to go wherever God sends, when He sends you, without being constrained by financial issues...

 … you must decide to uproot the belief that poverty equals holiness.

You can be wealthy, holy, set apart and madly in love with Jesus.

MYTH 3

Because I'm Older, I'm Stuck

"The best time to plant a tree was 20 years ago.
The second best time is now."

—Chinese Proverb

This is the belief that if you are older, if you are not caught up with the latest technologies, or have been financially stuck for a very long time, there is nothing you can do to get ahead. This myth isn't restricted to Christians, but I needed to address it because I hear it far too often from believers.

WHAT THIS PRODUCES

This produces Christians who have given up on changing the financial trajectory for their family. They feel it's too late to pursue the calling God has given them.

What's The Truth?

Let me share the story of a past client, let's call them the Smiths, a husband and wife in their early 60's. When the Smiths came to work with us, they believed there was no hope for their family's finances. They had been stuck in a cycle of lack for decades. They refinanced their home quite a few times, consolidated debts and tried to change their habits, increase their income and build something for their future but nothing had worked.

When they came to work with us, they told us they had tried budgeting and lowering their expenses but were still at the same place. They thought, let's just give this a shot. Within 4 weeks, for the *first* month in years, they had extra money at the end of the month sitting in their bank account. *And,* this was before we started working with them to increase their income.

In the next 4 weeks, his wife had increased her income at the same workplace and he doubled his income as well. Moreover, they changed their habits. They mastered the ability to keep their money instead of watching it slip through their fingers each month. This finally had them on a positive financial trajectory to paying off decades of debt and saving up for their nearing retirement.

I spoke with them about the changes they had seen. They explained that the biggest thing that surprised them was how different they were thinking. He kept on repeating, "It's become automatic," and, "I don't understand how but we're so different," and, "I am not even thinking about it, but somehow my mind is changing." His wife said, "It feels like there are new avenues in my brain that I never had before. The *urge* to shop is completely gone and I am so happy without it!"

A concern of hers had always been that the temporary joy

she received from spending would be gone. She said, "Toyin, I've always been a positive person and an encourager in my circles, but this is different. I'm happy at home. I'm grateful all the time and it is authentic without the stuff." Mind you, she said this *before* she increased her income.

Now they are no longer focused on trying to stay afloat financially each month. They have room in their minds to begin to build the vision God had given them years ago, for their specific way to add value to society.

I laughed so hard when they spoke of how automatic it was. I told them that's the wonderful science of how God has created our brain. The science community used to believe that once a person became an adult, their neural pathways were set for life; no more change. They used to believe you're stuck with whatever your parents and environment instilled in you growing up. So, if you have been in a cycle of success to lack again and again for years, there's nothing you can do about it. It's just your lot in life.

But that's not true! We have since learned that the brain continues to go through a process of neurogenesis throughout a person's lifetime and you are able to change your mind and therefore, your life, at any point. A friend once said, "you are one decision away from a completely different life."

It's completely understandable to feel stuck, especially if you have been actively trying to change your financial situation for *years*. It's easy to believe that because you've tried everything you know to do and haven't seen a change, nothing will work for you. While it's easy to believe this lie, those who do can never change. They don't give themselves the opportunity for a different experience.

In contrast, I spoke with another couple, also in their early 60's who said, "we know that nothing can help us anymore. Our plan is to live the rest of our lives with this load of debt, and thankfully when we die, our insurance will pay it off so that we're not passing it on to our children." Based on the average human lifespan, they still had about 15-20 years left to live, but in their hearts and minds, they had given up.

They didn't realize that even though they may escape paying that debt themselves, and they *may* save their kids from having to pay it on their behalf, they have also done something far more detrimental than not leaving a monetary burden behind. They have taught their children and grandchildren that when you keep trying and nothing seems to work, there's nothing you can do. That lesson is more costly than any bill. That lesson costs their children and grandchildren their future success if they don't take care to rebuild and learn outside of that influence.

Interestingly enough, Mr. Smith expressed the desire to live *longer* in one of our conversations as they began to see these changes. To some religious people, that may seem like an unspiritual desire. First, imagine living life in such a place of struggle and lack that you just want this part of your existence to be over to enjoy eternity with Jesus? Now, imagine what it means for that person to reconnect with God's purpose for them on this planet, at such a level, that they can honestly say like Paul, "to *live* is Christ, to die is gain" (Philippians 1:21).

He now has a purpose for the money that he is earning and is able to focus on adding value to society because he is no longer under extreme financial pressure.

Eternity will always be so much more than any experience this age has to offer. However, why choose to remain in a place of insignificance and struggle when you can apply a system that is proven to help you change.

It is not too late. You are not too old.

MYTH 4

I Can't Ask God For Things

For you have not received a spirit of slavery leading to fear
again, but you have received a spirit of adoption as sons by
which we cry out, "Abba! Father!"

— Romans 8:15

Many Christians are afraid of bringing their practical
needs and wants before God. They figure He can take
care of their spiritual needs like peace, joy, love or anything
else they consider spiritual like deliverance and healing. Yet,
when it comes to the temporal and earthly needs, they feel
they are on their own. They feel they have to figure things out
on their own and if things aren't working, well that's just
God's will.

WHAT THIS PRODUCES

This produces Christians who behave like slaves instead

of children of God. They do His work and figure He will reward them in eternity but ignore their needs in the present. It produces Christians who feel guilty for desiring things they may need like rest, a car, a house or a new furnace.

WHAT'S THE TRUTH?

In Chapter 1, I shared what happened to us around October 2017. The instability in that season, coupled with dealing with a property management company that lacked integrity, meant that we were forced to move seven times in seven months. While four of those times were due to their actions and the circumstances were out of our control, if we had enough extra money at the time, our family would not have been at their mercy.

About three days after our seventh move, I had a miscarriage and lost our second baby. After processing the grief, and while on bed rest recovering physically, I made a request to Abba. I asked Him to strengthen, settle and establish us in a home of our own.

> *"After you have suffered for a little while, the God of all grace, who called you to His eternal glory in Christ, will Himself perfect, confirm, strengthen and establish you."*
> 1 Peter 5:10

I set a goal to purchase our own home. A place where we could settle down, raise our kids and continue to do the work that God had called us to do. A friend knew about my goal and saw all the changes that were happening in my mindset and income. As you know this was the same season I had finally woken up and created the *Money Mindset SHIFT.* program for myself.

Soon after, she told me I may be too focused on getting this house. She told me, that she was, "more content to have the Giver than any gift." She then said, "I don't care if He never gives me a house, a car or anything at all. All I want is Him." I knew she had said this because she loves me and wanted me to stay on track. Thankfully, that was one of my last conversations before I went into my annual solitary seven-day prayer retreat and l was going to have ample time with Him. One of the first questions I asked the Holy Spirit was, "Am I off track in asking you for this house?"

When I first got saved, I was steeped in the love of money. That was part of what led to me having the debt in the first place. During my teenage years, I had more money pass through my hands than most would have by their twenties. God brought me into His kingdom and took the time to strip me of that love for money. He had me stop all my businesses, give away my car and all the other things I had taken pride in prior to knowing Him. This season of stripping me of the "stuff" externally culminated on the day He finally took their place in my heart.

Red Cars Made Me Cry

I had used my last three dollars to get to a prayer meeting at my alma mater. It was an amazing time worshipping God and praying with some brothers and sisters in Christ. Once the service was finished, we noticed that quite a few of us who had not attended the fellowship for a while were all there on that day. We spent some time reminiscing about the good ole' campus ministry days, sharing stories and jokes.

One of the guys in the group just bought a brand new red car and we were really happy for him. He mentioned that his red car matched that of another friend's in the group who recently purchased a new red car as well. We laughed at how random it was that they had both got the same type of car in the same span of time without talking to each other. We spoke about the days when we were in university and most of us had no cars. The few members of the group that did have cars, would drop the other members home. We spent some more time talking and laughing then parted ways. As we left the conversation and I headed toward the bus terminal, my mind was brimming with thoughts and memories.

I remembered those years of my life and how I used to be one of those who had a car and would spend hours dropping friends off all over the city after services. I remembered the $150,000 painting business I used to run while still in my teens and the thriving MLM business I had built. I remembered how since then, God told me to step out of business because of my desire for money and comfort. I remembered how He convicted me about my spending as I aimed to come out of debt. He led me to give my car away in order to save more money to put toward my goal of debt freedom. I thought of the work God had been doing to humble me financially and break off the god of Mammon from my heart.

As soon as I got to the bus stop, I realized that I had no fare to take the bus to my overnight work shift that night. There was nothing I could do about it. I was not living at home, so I couldn't run to my parents' room and grab some change or to one of my sisters to give me some cash. I knew that unless I did something quickly, I would not be on time for work.

As a last resort, I called one of my friends from the group, told him that I did not have the $3.00 to take the bus and asked if he was able to give me that amount. He immediately said he would, ran to the bus stop I was at and gave me $6.00 instead so that I could get back home after work.

I wish I could say I was gushing with gratitude to Abba

for providing for me just on time. Instead, I started to think of my Egypt. I reminisced about the "financial freedom" I had when money was my god. I remembered how I didn't just have enough to maintain a car but had even bought a car for my then boyfriend.

From the age of 16, I had always driven my own cars. Now, I was a University graduate and unable to afford bus fare. I had spent the year seeking God in a lifestyle of prayer and ministry while "my mates", as my Nigerian people would say, were getting on with their careers and making the type of money people went to University to be able to make.

I began to grow bitter in my heart with comparison and what ifs. I could see the state of my heart and it was ugly. I did not want to care so much, but I did. I arrived for my night-shift at work and called Josh, whom, back then was one of my best friends absolutely broken about the state of my heart. I shared with him what I had experienced that evening. I also shared how frustrated I was that I cared so much about it. He shared his frustration at not being able to help me in that season either, as God had directed him to stop his full-time job to seek Him, and serve Him full-time in a few ministries throughout the week and on the weekends.

It is one thing to complete an act of obedience and let go physically of what God tells you to release but that doesn't always mean your heart has let go of it. This was the conundrum I was in. I wanted to be free from the desire for comfort especially when it conflicted with my obedience to the Lord.

As I spoke to Joshua, he began to pray and I joined him in prayer. We were asking God to give us His heart about our finances, that we would see from His perspective and that we would trust Him completely. I was okay with these prayers. He then prayed a prayer that made me pause. He said, "God, bring us to a place where, if we never in our lives own another car, if we never buy a house, if we never have the things equivalent to this, we are still content in You. Help us to value You above it all."

Now, I had never in my born-again life considered the option of God in His providence deciding that I did not need a car or a house. At that moment, I realized that much of my sacrifice and service in those years had been with an unspoken agreement that in due season, the Lord would repay me, abundantly, in this life, with cars and houses. Or at least one of each. And good ones too. I didn't realize my heart had banked on this. So even though I had given away my car, I completely expected Him to give me a lot more in return. I expected Him to give me a great house and to make sure that at some point in my life I was able to live affluently, especially for all my voluntary discomfort.

My motivation for embracing sacrifice in that season was based on my desire for future comfort and not simply obeying and trusting Him. This was wrong because I realized at that moment that if my heart did not change, and He chose not to give me these things, after all, I would be offended at Him. In Matthew 11:6, Jesus said to John the Baptist, through his disciples, *"Blessed is he who is not offended at Me"*.

So many of us have hearts that are offended at God because we do not feel He has been fair to the suffering in our lives. We feel as though suffering and challenges have come with no relief. My head knew that God is better than fair. He is all wise and all powerful. If God was fair, we would all be going to hell. Yet He is wise, loving and abounding in mercy.

I spent the rest of that night shift, asking God to take that security that I had in future cars and houses and place it firmly in Him. I wanted Him to be my only hope in life. That whether I had things that made life easier or I struggled all my life, I would be content and fully satisfied in my Father and in the relationship and access that I had with Him.

He did surgery on my heart and removed that security I had found in things. Seven years later, we still believe and live that daily. There isn't enough time to detail all the stories of how we have obeyed God as a family despite the physical cost. This is why He could and still sends us wherever He chooses and we pick up our family and go whether is to a different country or to a different community.

BACK TO THE PRESENT

My biggest concern while building my business and getting financially stable was returning to a place where I needed "stuff" to make me happy or put my personal comfort above obedience to His will. So during this retreat, I asked Him to search my heart and correct me if I was wrong to ask Him for this house and actually plan towards purchasing it.

In my time of prayer, He reminded me of that story I told you to highlight that I am not the same Toyin that pursued money and things before I knew Him. He warned me of going from one extreme - the pursuit of money/things to the other - fear of money/things - and told me to read the story of the Prodigal Son in Luke 15: 11-32. And it said,

"A man had two sons. The younger of them said to his father, 'Father, give me the share of the estate that falls to me.' So he divided his wealth between them. And not many days later, the younger son gathered everything together and went on a journey into a distant country, and there he squandered his estate with loose living.

Now when he had spent everything, a severe famine occurred in that country, and he began to be impoverished. So he went and hired himself out to one of the citizens of that country, and he sent him into his fields to feed swine. And he would have gladly filled his stomach with the pods that the swine were eating, and no one was giving anything to him.

But when he came to his senses, he said, 'How many of my father's hired men have more than enough bread, but I am dying here with hunger! I will get up and go to my father, and will say to him, "Father, I have sinned against heaven, and in your sight; I am no longer worthy to be called your son; make me as one of your hired men."'

So he got up and came to his father. But while he was still a long way off, his father saw him and felt compassion for him, and ran and embraced him and kissed him. And the son said to him, 'Father, I have sinned against heaven and in your sight; I am no longer worthy to be called your son.' But the father said to his slaves, *'Quickly bring out the best robe and put it on him, and put a ring on his hand and sandals on his feet; and bring the fattened calf, kill it, and let us eat and celebrate; for this son of mine was dead and has come to life again; he was lost and has been found.'* And they began to celebrate.

"Now his older son was in the field, and when he came and approached the house, he heard music and dancing. And he summoned one of the servants and began inquiring what these things could be. And he said to him, 'Your brother has come, and your father has killed the fattened calf because he has received him back safe and sound.'

But he became angry and was not willing to go in; and his father came out and began pleading with him. But he answered and said to his father, 'Look! For so many years I have been serving you and I have never neglected a command of yours; and yet *you have never given me a young goat, so that I might celebrate with my friends; but when this son of yours came, who has devoured your wealth with prostitutes, you killed the fattened calf for him.'*

And he said to him, '**Son, you have always been with me, and all that is mine is yours.** But we had to celebrate and rejoice, for this brother of yours was dead and has begun to live, and was lost and has been found.'"

God began to explain a part of this parable I had not previously noticed. The older son had access to his father and could have asked for the fatted calf at any time but he had more of a *slave* mentality than a son. Meanwhile, the prodigal son knew his father enough to understand that even though he had committed such an unthinkable thing against him, his dad would love him, show him mercy and receive him back into his house, even if as one of the servants.

Yet, the son who stayed faithful to the dad the entire time thought of his dad as a hard taskmaster. Someone he worked for, who provided for his basic needs but not someone he could approach to ask for something as unnecessary as a calf for a party.

My Earthly Father

God also reminded me of the day I was graduating from University. While scholarships had covered most of my tuition, in that final year I was $1000 short. I approached my dad to ask him if he would give me the $1,000. He could tell that I was extremely nervous about whatever I was about to ask him for.

After getting the words out of my mouth, my dad asked

me, "Why did it take you so long to ask me for this? You're my daughter. You live under my roof and your education is my responsibility. If you had asked me for this much earlier I would have given it to you." He went ahead and paid the final $1,000 without any fuss. I remembered thinking, wow, here I was berating myself for needing his help, but he's my dad and he was happy to chip in.

Abba said to me, "Toyin, you went through an ordeal with housing that has cost you dearly. You stayed close to Me throughout and asked me for a house and stability for your children. That is a relationship between a Father and His daughter. It is okay to ask. I could say no, but I said yes. It is my pleasure to give you good gifts" (Matthew 7:7-11, James 1:17, Psalm 23:1).

I'm not saying that everyone who reads this should ask Abba for what I asked. What I am saying is this, God cares about your everyday life. You commune with Him spiritually but He knows that you need to eat physical food. He knows that some of you have been working extremely hard for a very long time and would like a break, like some vacation time. He knows you need to pay off that debt. He knows you need to have money saved for coming projects. He not only knows what you need, He knows what you want.

You don't have to pretend to be so spiritual that you won't speak to God about your practical needs and wants. A relationship is based on communication. He already knows what you have need of. Talking to Him about them does not automatically mean you have put those things above Him. It also does not mean He will give you everything you want, but part of the relationship is maintaining an open line of communication.

Here's the truth: when you are free to talk to God about your goals and financial dreams, you get to pursue those goals and dreams *with* Him! You will be able to tap into His wisdom which brings His supernatural activity into your planning and thinking process. You are His son/daughter. If you need something, ask Him. Do not feel like you have to hide behind His back to get your finances on track. If He *does not* want you to have that thing and you are open to hearing His voice, He will let you know! It is a conversation. This is relationship.

One Caveat

Let me remind you that building wealth as a Christian is not primarily about the money or your comfort. It is 100% about living out the purpose God has called you to. So desiring things cannot be your primary reason for desiring financial freedom. Your vision and goal must always be to advance His kingdom and purposes on this earth.

You've heard much about our years of struggling financially. Even when we were unsure about what we would eat and paying our rent, it never stole our joy. You can watch some of our family vlogs in that season on YouTube. Recently we tried to find photos of these seasons in particular and noticed that we were beaming even in the toughest of times.

We were content and satisfied in His goodness to us in so many areas, even when our lack led to the miscarriage. While we do not believe He caused it, we could see about six distinct ways He cushioned the blow and helped us through that season supernaturally. Not having enough finances also didn't stop us from obeying Him wherever He sent us or serving the people He sent to us with what we had at that point.

It didn't stop us from having fun. Even in the year and a half we had no couch and sat on an air mattress in our home, we had a Christmas party (it was a Bring Your Own Chair potluck), and were unashamed of where He had us. By God's grace, we had learned to ground our joy and peace in Him through the things we had already suffered (Phil. 4:12). If you have not first come to that place, that should be the foundation of your journey to financial freedom. If we measure your lives by what we have or don't, how different are we from those who don't have eternal life?

"Everyone who has something should behave as if he or she has nothing."
2 Cor. 6:10

If you are depending on material things to give you peace or joy, whether you have those things or not, you have a love of money. Whatever you have is completely His and He can do with it whatever He desires, whenever He chooses. This is a tricky myth because you can easily get caught in either of the extremes. **I encourage you at this point to take some time and ask Abba where you are at.**

- Are you putting your hope and trust in the things you are surrounded by?
- Are you waiting for when you receive specific things from God before you will really be happy?
- Are you afraid of having anything because you feel it will mean you don't really love and value the Giver?
- Do you hide your desires from Him or think that He does not care about your needs and wants?
- Is your relationship with God open and free in the area of finances? Do you talk to Him about your goals and dreams? Do you know what He desires for you financially?

MYTH 5

God Loves Me So It Has To Work Out

God displayed his love for Noah when He directed him to build the ark. If Noah ignored that instruction, he could not accuse God of leaving them there to drown.

— Toyin Crandell

The most heartbreaking part of my sessions is seeing the years of pain that a negative relationship with money causes in families, relationships, marriages, children and work. It is heartbreaking to see that even after all the pain it has caused, some chalk the solution up to,

"Things will change because God is good and loves me. It just has to change."

"God loves me and provides for me and so I don't need to worry about my finances because it'll all work out."

"I just know things will get better. They *have* to get better."

"I refuse to concern myself with my finances. God is going to take care of me."

"The bible says I shouldn't worry for tomorrow, that tomorrow will take care of itself."

Usually, this isn't said in the context of taking action but as a cushion, a reason to maintain their hands-off approach to changing their financial situation. They have moved the responsibility of caring for their family or living the life God has purposed for them, from themselves to God. There is no ownership of the situation.

When a person refuses responsibility and offshores the weight of change from them to God, they're expecting Jesus to step down from heaven, walk into the bank and pay off that debt on their behalf.

I have had people tell me similar versions of this, "Toyin, it's a miracle I heard about you! Last night, I was literally in tears, crying and telling God that I need help. I don't know what to do or how to change. The next day, I saw a post from you on Facebook (or saw you on a TV or other show). I felt Him nudge me to go ahead and watch one of your webinars, and I booked this session with you. I know that God wants to set me up to win."

I always take this level of excitement and conviction with a grain of salt because I have seen time and time again, that being a victim is comfortable and the discomfort of deciding to change is most times, more than most people are willing to bear. I would speak with this type of person, tell them what it takes to shift out of financial struggle and into success. Unfortunately, 7 times out of 10, they are unwilling to take action because they feel God will one day do the work *for* them.

It reminds me of a story my father used to tell us as children:

"A man was stuck on his rooftop in a flood. He was praying to God for help. Soon a man in a rowboat came by and the fellow shouted to the man on the roof, "Jump in, I can save you." The stranded fellow shouted back, "No, it's ok, I'm praying to God and he is going to save me." So the rowboat went on.

Then a motorboat came by. "The fellow in the motorboat shouted, "Jump in, I can save you."

To this, the stranded man said, "No thanks, I'm praying to God and he is going to save me. I have faith." So the motorboat went on.

Then a helicopter came by and the pilot shouted down, "Grab this rope and I will lift you to safety."

To this, the stranded man again replied, "No thanks, I'm praying to God and he is going to save me. I have faith." So the helicopter reluctantly flew away.

Soon the water rose above the rooftop and the man drowned. He went to Heaven. He finally got his chance to discuss this whole situation with God, at which point he exclaimed, "I had faith in you but you didn't save me, you let me drown. I don't understand why!"

To this God replied, "I sent you a rowboat and a motorboat and a helicopter, what more did you expect?"

I see this happen every. single. day. I have had some people call me back years later saying, "Things are worse than before, the debt is larger, my responsibilities have grown: what can I do now?"

WHAT THIS PRODUCES

This produces Christians who are in line for an irreversible nightmare of a wake-up call in the latter years of their lives if they do not change their trajectory right now.

WHAT'S THE TRUTH?

Guess what? There is no rewind button in retirement and old age. Yes, God may provide a miracle to care for you when you are no longer able to work but being at the mercy of the government's social net is just about the worst plan you can have. I have had heartbreaking conversations with a few men and women far into their retirement years who genuinely believed that things would change simply because God is good. Some of them are still loaded with crushing debt, many are living on meager pensions and barely able to buy groceries each month. There are people who are waiting to pass away so that they don't have to deal with all of this stress anymore.

Maybe you are one of them or know someone like this. Whenever we can give helpful advice or connect them to resources that are available to them, we do. But more than anything, these conversations in particular motivate me to cut through the baseless optimism and tell people the truth while they still have time to do something about it.

Yes, God loves you immensely and because of that, He will not do your part. If a child is to learn how to walk, and a parent carries them everywhere because that child doesn't know how to walk; the child will never learn for themselves. If that parent allows the child to grow into adulthood without ever giving them the opportunity to learn how to walk, we would call that abuse.

That is not love. In the love and mercy of God, He did not just pay off my debt for me. In His love, He did not allow my business to succeed when I had not changed internally or invested in myself to learn how to run a successful business.

In His love, He sent me to people who knew more than I did and challenged me to get humble, empty my cup and learn.

This was a necessary process for me to step into His full purpose for me. He didn't sit in on my sessions with my mentors for me. He didn't read the 150+ books I have studied to learn what I now know. He didn't ask the questions I needed to ask my mentors for me. He didn't purchase the hundreds of thousands of dollars worth of coaching I have invested in. No, I had to do it. Not Him.

David and Goliath

We often talk about David's faith in the fight against Goliath. I've heard many sermons of the 5 stones David picked up representing each letter of the word "F-A-I-T-H". But guess what? David did not kill Goliath with "faith" alone. David killed Goliath by stepping out *in* faith *with* action. If he did not run towards the giant swinging his sling and stone, the giant would not have fallen because of his confidence in God's love.

In fact, if David had not practiced using that sling and stone to kill lions and bears, a sling and stone would have been useless to him when facing Goliath. He used practical skills he cultivated during his time of preparation, to defeat Goliath and bring glory to God.

Noah's Ark

Likewise, Noah worked on the Ark for years and years in order to save his family and all the animals in creation. He did not say, "If God loves me enough to warn me about the flood ahead of time, He'll definitely take care of me. After all, I have a relationship with Him and I hear from Him, so I know for sure that when that flood comes we will be cared for." No.

When he was made aware, he took day after painstaking day, building a massive boat in a generation where they had never before seen rain. He was ridiculed, ostracized and laughed at... until the rain began. He invested physical effort and his belief in the promise of protection from God was proven by his obedience in taking the action necessary for that protection.

God displayed his love for Noah and his family when He directed him to build the ark! If he ignored that instruction, it would not have changed how much God loved him, but he could not accuse God of leaving them there to drown. In the same way, God gives us instruction about our finances. It is up to us to listen and take action.

DO NOT WORRY ABOUT TOMORROW

"For this reason I say to you, do not be *worried* about your life, as to what you will eat or what you will drink; nor for your body, as to what you will put on. Is not life more than food, and the body more than clothing?

Look at the birds of the air, that they do not sow, nor reap nor gather into barns, and yet your heavenly Father feeds them. Are you not worth much more than they? And who of you by being *worried* can add a single hour to his life? And why are you *worried* about clothing?

Observe how the lilies of the field grow; they do not toil nor do they spin, yet I say to you that not even Solomon in all his glory clothed himself like one of these. But if God so clothes the grass of the field, which is alive today and to-morrow is thrown into the furnace, will He not much more clothe you? You of little faith!

Do not *worry* then, saying, 'What will we eat?' or 'What will we drink?' or 'What will we wear for clothing?' For the Gentiles eagerly seek all these things; for your heavenly Father knows that you need all these things.

But seek first His kingdom and His righteousness, and all

these things will be added to you. "So do not *worry* about to-morrow; for tomorrow will care for itself. Each day has enough trouble of its own."

Matthew 6:25-34

You will note that throughout this passage, God said do not *worry* about your finances, He didn't say do not think or plan.

Many people spend time worrying about their finances but never any time doing something to change it. You need to treat every opportunity like your last. You can't just say you want something. You have the opportunity and access to make things happen, so do it! Wake up and take advantage of today. You only get this day in this month, this year once. What are you going to do today to step outside of your financial comfort zone and sow into your future?

Love is when God gives you opportunities to build your own muscle of financial understanding and apply what you learn. Many people don't want to attempt that journey because financial change is most difficult in the beginning and the thought of committing to the vision they have for their lives triggers layers of fear. Fear of failure, fear of being embarrassed, fear of rejection or being different, fear of success, **fear of anything that isn't their passive way of life, because the victim story feels more familiar.**

Your change is possible but God will not do your part. He loves you enough to get this book into your hands. Don't wait until you have no food as I did. Don't wait until you're too old to work any longer. Don't wait until your business has to close down from lack of profitability. Don't wait until you lose the job. You owe it to yourself, your children and theirs to invest in changing your life today so that the cycle of lack or "almost" succeeding ends with you.

A faith declaration for your finances without a goal and clear action plan is a disappointment waiting to happen.

MYTH 6

If I'm Financially Free I Won't Trust God

How blessed is the man who fears the Lord...
Wealth and riches are in his house,
And his righteousness endures forever...
His heart is steadfast, *trusting in the Lord.*

— Psalm 112: 1,3 7

This can be a very real fear those of us who treasure our relationship with God above everything else. We do not want the comforts or conveniences of this life to take away from our dependence on God.

WHAT THIS PRODUCES

This means that for a lot of people who are truly given to the will of God, they will do anything He tells them to do when it results in difficulty, hardship. On the other hand, if God ever desires to bless them financially, they think it is a plot of the devil to take them away from Him. This means some of the most giving people on this earth are left unable to help others the way that they have been called to.

WHAT'S THE TRUTH?

I'll be honest with you, this was a belief that really held me back when I shifted into the marketplace. In Myth 4, I shared with you my financial past before I knew Christ: how I loved money and found security in it. I also shared my subsequent season of doing away with any physical attachment to money.

In that place, I learned to really trust God and saw Him come through consistently in my most desperate situations. I had built such a rich history with God and somehow thought that if I had my bills paid, savings in the bank and investments that are working for me, I would lose that dependence on God which I valued so much.

While going through this process of allowing God to search my heart and mind on finances, He showed me that I was afraid of financial success because I did not want my heart to grow cold toward Him. He said to me, "Why do you think you will lose Me if you have money?" He sent me to the following scriptures:

"And this is the will of God, that I should not lose even one of all those he has given me, but that I should raise them up at the last day. For it is my Father's will that all who see his Son and believe in him should have eternal life. I will raise them up at the last day."
John 6:39-40

"...And I come to You. Holy Father, keep them in Your name, the name which You have given Me, that they may be one even as We are. While I was with them, I was keeping them in Your name which You

have given Me; and I guarded them and not one of them perished but the son of perdition, so that the Scripture would be fulfilled... "I am praying not only for these disciples but also for all who will ever believe in me through their message."

John 17:11-12, 20

He began to teach me that my walk and faith in Him is not a work of my own. It is self-righteous of us to think that we are the author and finisher of our own faith. Some have departed from the Lord with no money just as others have with plenty of it. At all times, the faith we have in God is a precious amazing gift of grace and is not our works so we cannot boast about it!

If God was willing to fight for your heart when you were a sinner, running away from Him, doing your own thing and drowning in your mess, why would He stop fighting for your heart now that you are fully committed to Him? Why would He send you into the marketplace in your career or business to set you up for eternal failure?

I have learned from years of following and learning from Jesus about obedience that if you continuously ignore God's instruction for whatever reason, your heart will grow cold regardless of whether you have money or not!

If He says it's time to get your finances in order and you ignore His direction, that action of disobedience bleeds into other areas of your life.

He told me it was time to stop shortchanging the mission He had given me and to take what I was teaching to individual persons and learn to create systems that would allow me to teach hundreds and thousands at a time. It was time to study in the field in order to give and serve at my best. It was time to humble myself and learn how to run my business in fiscal excellence. I also needed to make sure my family was fed so I could focus on the mission. If I was to fulfill His calling on my life, I had to get serious.

More than anything, challenging this myth forced me to trust God with my spiritual walk. I personally did not know what it would look like for me not to spend hours each day in prayer and worship like my days of full-time ministry. When I was willing to trust God with my relationship with Him, He was able to show me the other side of the picture.

It is interesting, the more we have matured financially as a family, the more we recognize it has only been the power and hand of God.

God is our Source. When I say that, I don't just mean our source of financial provision. He has confirmed even in this season that He is our source of wisdom, love, joy, peace, wisdom, creativity, physical strength, grace, mercy and did I say wisdom? Every good and perfect gift comes from the Father of lights with whom there is no variation or shadow of turning (James 1:17). That verse wasn't pulled from an internet source, it's been burned into my heart.

Flexibility and Gratitude

I once gifted a friend two of my worship albums, *"Declaration of Dependence"* and *"Broken Spirit, Contrite Heart"*. I visited her office a few weeks later and heard one of the albums playing softly in the background. She mentioned that she had a practice of consistently playing worship music in her office. This is a way she practices connecting with Abba at all times and my albums just happened to have become the worship music of choice. I noted to myself, that the reason she was free to cultivate this peaceful, worshipful atmosphere was because she's built a phenomenal business and that office space was *hers!*

Because of the flexibility of running my own business, I can devote *more* time now than before to seeking Him. Also, in dedicating a lot more time to my business, I've been able to create a consistent routine of seeking Him in prayer and the word. This is something I've desperately wanted and needed for years in my walk with God. It's almost backward!

When I didn't have the added pressure of expertly managing my time, my time with Him was sporadic though beautiful, when I got to it. Now, because I know how much I need Him to sustain my life, family, business, everything, I cannot skip my time with Him every morning. I am free to take a few afternoons each week in worship, song, and dance to Him.

Moreover, I have learned gratitude and trust on a level that I never grasped before. I wake up and go to sleep overflowing with gratitude and thankfulness for God's grace each day. It hasn't necessarily been related to the actual financial growth but to see His ability to change my heart and to help me change the story for thousands of people. To witness these "miracles" of His provision and breakthrough in their lives reminds me that it is because they have partnered with God's plan for their lives.

You better believe we've had sacrificial seasons even on this side of our financial experience, but stepping out and trusting Him through it all has taught me how present He is through the good and bad. Like Tauren Wells sings, He is both the God of the *hills* as well as a God of the *valleys*.

Just like I said in Chapter 3, money simply amplifies what is in your heart. If you are grateful to God, it will increase your level of gratitude. If you love Him above anything else, it will push you into deeper places of communion with Him. If you trust Him, money will teach you to trust Him for more of His will. If you treasure His presence, it will allow you to prioritize it even more. If you want to serve and do mission work, having extra money frees you up to do that in a more focused way. If you enjoy your family, you are freed up to spend more time with them.

In building a real relationship with God I learned to trust Him for everything. I knew I wouldn't have my basic necessities without His daily provision. That reality hasn't disappeared because things are not as tight financially. Still today, I wouldn't have anything without His daily provision. I cannot run my business, balance my work life with being a good wife and mother, do anything that I am doing without His grace. Even the wisdom for the numerous situations I assist people with daily are only addressed through His wisdom.

In every season, I trust God because I am desperate and cannot live life without His daily presence.

I'll be honest. I'm still not as perfect or consistent as I would like to be. And I need to be reminded by Him at least twice a year to remember the more important things just as He did when I was occupied with ministry work. But that is the nature of the human heart. We are prone to wander, yet He is faithful to always bring us back to what matters most.

He will not let you go if you remain open and hungry for Him. He will not let you go if you stay focused on the eternal significance of what He has called you to do in your workplace.

Being financially free will not remove the need for your trust in God. If you trust and depend on Him, being financially free will only amplify that.

MYTH 7

It's More Holy To Think Small

"One who is faithful in a very little is also faithful in much, and one who is dishonest in a very little is also dishonest in much."

— Luke 16:10 (ESV)

Many Christians are told that if they push for big dreams, they are trying to build their own kingdom and not God's. They choose to live below their God-given potential for earning income or building wealth because they don't want to seem like they're building something for themselves.

WHAT THIS PRODUCES

This produces Christians who don't want to dream big for fear of looking like they are being overly ambitious. They don't want to seem like their goals are self-focused so they pretend they haven't been given a bigger mission and stay small in order to look humble.

What's The Truth?

The truth is obedience to God in everything is what is most important. If Paul was afraid of reaching multitudes of people because he didn't want to seem ambitious, he wouldn't have spread the gospel as virally as he did. He was taken by a vision: to make Jesus known to the Gentiles.

Today, there are many different ways to bring the kingdom of God to those who need Him. The marketplace is one of the most open spaces to speak to those who do not yet know God, not the church. You find more people who are looking for answers to life's questions at work than you will at church! If we truly have the best news on the planet, which I believe we do, why are we so content with keeping it a secret?

You may have noticed that I emphasized my goal of empowering at least 1 million people through this book. I want to do my part in helping them overcome their limiting mindsets and taking their place as financial pillars in God's kingdom. I had people criticize me for thinking this big especially when I began to study social media marketing. Why was it wrong to learn the language of our generation so that we could actually get a message out? We were tracking our numbers, the people who were hearing the message and I continued to apply what I had learned through marketing so that more people could receive our message in ministry and later on, in my business.

Why Do We Tell Each Other to Dream Small?

I understand focusing on the one. I promise you. I've had more opportunities to focus on the individual while growing my business than I ever had building for "small". I have the opportunity to speak to hundreds of people each year who are not clients of mine. I speak to them for at least a full hour, sometimes up to 3 hours, for free, helping them find clarity about their current financial situation and setting them up for success moving forward.

For each person in those free sessions, that conversation is life changing. At that moment, they are "the one". And I don't sit back patting myself on the back for having reached out to 25 last week, I look to find more ways to reach more people who need a financial breakthrough.

Yes, I have had seasons where God has told me to rein things in, rest, even do nothing at all. I had another season where I organized a ladies bible study and poured everything I had into a few ladies. Those women are still some of my favourite people on the planet and I may run a bible study again if God leads me to. As drastically as their lives and relationships with God grew in that season of our lives, I am now able to bring that message to many more than the few women I started with.

It's all the same Toyin, with the same Jesus, only reaching more people. And you don't need to apologize for aiming for more either.

Jesus gave everything He had when He was here on the earth. He spoke to multitudes and taught them about the kingdom of God. While they didn't have microphones and other amplification systems to project his voice, he used the tools available to Him get more people to hear the message. He would sit in the boat on the water and allow the dynamics of the sea to carry his voice farther than speaking on land. He would walk high up a mountain (see Matthew 5) one of the reasons may have been because it projected his voice much better than speaking from the bottom.

So why do we as Christians fear technology? Why are we so afraid of getting this good news to people who need it? If Jesus worked smart, I will work smart. If Jesus knew how to amplify the message He had been given, I will do everything in my power to get the word out about His love and saving grace. I will work smarter and not harder.

If Jesus died on the cross and asked God for the *world* to be saved, COME ON! I will give my life to reach 1 million of the *billions* that need Him.

Paul traveled across Asia to see as many people saved as possible. He didn't take credit for the churches. They didn't have to be named "the church of Paul". All he wanted was for people who had never heard of Jesus Christ to receive an invitation into God's kingdom and be saved from the punishment of their own sins. All the apostles blazed with the same fire. They taught, travelled, worked, lived and died that more and more people would receive the truth.

If your business is being run with integrity and you will use wealth to build communities and transform lives, why should you think it more holy to play small? There are so many missionaries who are trying to focus on the work of sharing the gospel but are held back because of a lack of finances. They do not have time to go into the marketplace. If you have been sent into the marketplace, why not maximize your opportunity there and use what you earn to spread the work of the gospel. Why not set a goal to give at least one million dollars to the work of the kingdom?

I know so many business owners who do just that. Individuals who run businesses with integrity, give more than you can imagine to causes focused on ending poverty in the world, assisting persecuted Christians globally and the like.

You can also dream big to assist your customers! Unfortunately, there are people out there who really do just care for the money. People will cheat, lie and steal to get it. If you are not in that group, why would you leave the bulk of your customer base to those who will take advantage of them? You are *needed*!

I'm not saying that everyone needs to reach 1 million people with the message God has given them. I am saying that whether you have been called to 50, 500 or 5 million, there is no part that is less than the others and nothing to be ashamed of! We need to stop running to extremes. Some only respect a ministry based on the size of its reach and focus on things like how many people got saved at your evangelistic outreach. While others despise large scale ministries and say, "look at that Pastor with the megachurch, he's just trying to build his own kingdom." Listen, we need everyone's hand on deck and no one is more spiritual than the other.

The point of addressing this myth is to be willing to do whatever God tells you to do even if it looks obnoxious to other Christians. And for those who may not be called to impacting thousands to understand that that is not a selfish thing.

For the purposes of this book, I am here to remind you that you do not have to feel guilty about setting a *big* goal to impact people positively for the sake of the gospel!

MYTH 8

I Am Too Broke To Tithe

Trust in the Lord with all your heart
And do not lean on your own understanding.
In all your ways acknowledge Him,
And He will make your paths straight.

— Proverbs 3:5-6

Some of you have been in such a tight place financially you have started to think: what's the point of tithing? How can I find the extra money to give to God each month when I can barely cover my basic bills?

WHAT THIS PRODUCES

This produces Christians who have disconnected their financial journey from God in a trusting and practical level. I believe it is a place of trying to get this done on their own even though they may be praying for change to happen. WHAT'S THE TRUTH?

"Then I will rebuke the devourer for you…"
Malachi 3:11

Often, people tell me that they encounter random "emergencies" in their finances. For example, they save money and every single time, something happens to bring them back to ground zero. Suddenly, the car breaks down needing repairs equal to what they saved, or there is a health emergency and so on. One woman in the space of 2 years had a few car accidents, a house fire, a flood, and other smaller emergencies. While, you may not have had that level of attack, back to back, many of us have endured the bitter taste of the devourer coming in. Our hard-earned fruit is stolen before we can enjoy it with our families or use it for it's God's intended purpose.

Whenever someone tells me about consistent financial emergencies taking place in their lives, I know there is almost always one of two things taking place.

- They do not tithe.
- They tithe but live in a constant state of negative expectation that they don't know how to shake. Call it trusting firmly in Murphy's Law.

In this space, I will only address tithing. As I get into this discussion, let me make this clear, I am not a pastor of a church and I don't plan on becoming one. Tithing is not about your church. Tithing is not about your pastor. Tithing is about tapping into a principle and covenant that God has made available to you as His child. Period.

"Bring the whole tithe into the storehouse, so that there may be food

in My house, and test Me now in this," says the Lord of hosts, "if I
will not open for you the windows of heaven and pour out for you a
blessing until it overflows. Then I will rebuke the devourer for you, so
that it will not destroy the fruits of the ground; nor will your vine in
the field cast its grapes," says the Lord of hosts.
"All the nations will call you blessed, for you shall be a delightful
land," says the Lord of hosts."
Malachi 3:10-12

You Owe God 100%, not 10%

My dad once told me a story. He was on a cruise and he
had the opportunity to observe this young family. The father
had served a wonderful breakfast for his young son from the
buffet. At one point, he asked his son for a bite from his eggs
and the son made a huge fuss and refused to share. My dad
watched this all happen and immediately God showed him the
parallel between many of His children and that little boy.

- They were sitting in a buffet where there was unlimited
  food.
- The father could have gotten what he needed at any
  time he wanted. He wasn't starving.
- The boy couldn't reach for the food and couldn't prepare his own plate. He was completely dependent on
  his father for any part of his meal.
- The father could have easily taken away the full plate
  and left that boy with nothing to eat.
- He could have forcefully taken the eggs from the plate
  (he was bigger and stronger).
- He allowed his son to believe that he owned that plate
  and eat to his heart's content.

While people are busy criticizing and attacking the idea of
tithing, remember that God has given you 100% of anything

you have to your name.

- Without the strength and ability from God…
- Without breath in your lungs (also from God)…
- Without wisdom, creativity and the ability to think…
- Without His overarching grace and favour…
- Without His provision in your life…

What would you have in your pocket? What would you have in your bank account? Billy Graham once said, "Give me five minutes with a person's checkbook, and I will tell you where their heart is." This cannot be more easily seen than in a person's commitment to tithing.

But Toyin, What About The Pastors That Misuse Tithe?

Some people busy themselves with searching out pastors or leaders who are caught misusing tithes and making a large show of the few while ignoring the majority of pastors and church leaders who live under the fear of God and honour God in their use of church funds.

They focus on the few that abuse tithe and use that as an excuse for not tithing personally. They think that they are "getting back" at those pastors. They don't know that they are setting themselves up for a financial loss which will only affect themselves and their families.

When I give to my home church, I do not obsess with their decisions in how they use that money. If I do not trust the decision making process or heart of a pastor, it wouldn't be my home church in the first place! So, if God has led me to a church and I am willing to learn from that ministry and its leaders, then there is a basic level of trust I am giving them to use my tithe and others in a way that honours God.

Keep in mind that we will all be accountable to God for

how we use money. Pastors and church leaders are accountable to God for how they spend the tithe that comes in. I am accountable to God for obeying His word and doing my part in tithing.

TITHING VERSUS GIVING OFFERING

People often ask me about tithing to ministries or simply giving 10% to someone in need each month. You can always give to ministries and to those in need, but be committed to giving regularly to the church where you are planted and growing as well.

Many of you have been blessed by God with a generous heart. Giving has always been one of my greatest joys and was one of my biggest limitations in the early part of my debt and even financial freedom journey. If you are like me, you find joy in giving. You feel ecstatic being able to help family members and friends when they need it. You feel great when you get to help out at church or other charities you care about and see the difference your financial contribution makes.

That can eventually lead to a saviour complex where you begin to think:

- I am needed therefore I am loved.
- If I don't do it who will?
- I can't stop now, too many people need me.
- I don't want to lose the relationship if I say no.
- It's selfish of me to not help.
- God will pour back into me for all my giving.

To make things more complicated, you may have friends, family members, and organizations asking and expecting your time, your vested emotions and of course, your finances.

When teaching clients about debt freedom, I am careful

to explain the process of giving and tithing so that they understand how to do it in a balanced way. This way, they do not remain in debt as a way of "bribing God" and so that they do not overgive.

The wealth God has given you is not for you and your family alone. So yes, give extravagantly, but pay attention. There is seedtime and there is harvest. If you eat the seed, how can you expect it to grow?

The Double Whammy Weekend

I have tons of stories of God's supernatural protection of our finances because of this practice of tithing. However, there was one weekend in particular when we could not ignore it. We had begun our shift from financial struggle into abundance and had maintained our commitment to tithe during the process.

During that time, I was scheduled to speak at a conference in the heart of downtown Toronto. As I drove down the Gardiner Expressway, our car hit a pothole. There was a loud bang on impact and which led to this ongoing loud, grating sound. It did not matter what speed I was going. It only quieted at full stops.

I called my husband and told him what had happened. I didn't have time to find a mechanic as I was slated to be at this conference all day for two days.

On the second day, my husband drove down with me. He was concerned about the sound, my safety and out of urgency he decided to take it to a mechanic while I spoke. We didn't know any mechanics in that area so we would be completely at their mercy for pricing. He expected it to cost us a few hundred dollars if not more. I prayed out loud and said to God,

"Abba, You said that if we tithe faithfully, You would protect our finances from the devourer. I ask that this car would be fixed for free or very close to free in Jesus name!"

My husband gave me a funny look, but came into agreement and said, "Amen." We laughed and kissed goodbye.

He joined us mid-day so I knew the car had been fixed, which was a relief. On our way home in our back to normal, quiet car, I asked him, "By the way, how much did it cost?" He exclaimed, "$17!" I was shocked! This was the cheapest mechanic bill we ever had and the car has since been completely fine. We thanked God for protecting our finances and drove home.

When we arrived home, we couldn't find my husband's phone anywhere. He remembered that he had the phone in the parking garage where we parked in downtown. He also remembered placing it beside his coffee on top of the car while buckling our daughter in. He remembered taking the coffee into the car… but not the phone.

We realized that the loud bump we heard on the top of our car while driving on Gardiner Expressway that night, wasn't a random piece of snow or rock hitting our car from a nearby truck. It was most likely the sound of his phone bumping along the roof of our car, and it was likely lying in pieces on the highway. Really? We had paid that phone off and were on a great BYOD (bring your own device) plan with our phone company. Getting a new phone would cost us at least $1,000 whether in a contract or within our plan.

Automatically, I prayed the same prayer I had prayed that morning, "Abba, You said that You would protect our finances if we tithe, we have obeyed You and I ask that we would retrieve this phone with no issues tomorrow morning in Jesus name."

Now, the Gardiner Expressway is a 100km/hr highway. If the phone made it to the highway on our car, which wasn't a guarantee, the chances of it being safe were slim to nil. It could easily have been run over and even if it wasn't run over, if the phone was in the middle of the highway, we simply would not risk our lives for $1,000.

So we drove downtown once again, merged onto the Gardiner and I studied the road while my husband focused on driving. At one point I felt like this was a useless attempt. Suddenly, I saw a small black thing off on the shoulder of the highway. I told him to pull over. He pulled over and I quickly jumped out of the car (safe on the shoulder), ran a few metres to the black thing and sure enough, it was his phone, upside down.

I picked it up and ran back to the car. We flipped it over and to our shock, it was completely unscathed. There was a bit of dust but not one scratch to show the night it had. Once again, we thanked God profusely for protecting our finances in this double whammy attempted attack within one weekend.

This is just one of many stories I can tell you of close calls on our finances, where we remembered our covenant with God and activated it in a time of attack.

So, whenever the thought comes into your mind, "I'm too broke to tithe," you need to respond, "I'm too broke not to tithe."

MYTH 9

I Can "Pray, Tithe And Give" My Way Out Of Struggle

What use is it, my brethren, if someone says he has faith
but he has no works? Can that faith save him?

— James 1:14

Some of you read the last myth and probably thought that
does not apply to you since you have been faithfully tithing
but still there has been no change. A huge part of what I
learned growing up was to pray, tithe and give. I thought if
you pray, tithe and give, God will pour back into you.

For those who aren't Christians, you might think that if
you serve others, give and are a nice person, everything's going
to work out. I knew and practiced this principle even before
I was fully devoted to Christ. It was church 101.

When we were on the journey out of lack and into abundance, a millionaire mentor of mine, a born again Christian

and pastor said, "Praying, tithing and giving is not enough to build wealth."

Guys, I almost closed the conversation right there. I was like, "Um ... fall back, sir!" Then my husband Joshua and I started talking about it. We asked each other a question that I want to pose to you today:

How many people do you know personally who pray, tithe and give faithfully, but who live and die in debt, struggle, in lack or just enough?

The Canadian Payroll Association found that 37% of Canadians are overwhelmed by their debt and 47% would find it difficult to meet their financial obligations if their paycheck was delayed by one week. According to TD Bank, 27% of Canadians are not able to save any portion of their monthly income. RBC Bank stated in December 2017 that 75% of Canadians are in debt.

If you're reading from the USA, don't judge too quickly. The situation is similar, if not worse. According to a poll conducted by The Associated Press - NORC Center for Public Affairs Research in 2016, 66% of Americans would struggle to pay for a $1,000 emergency and 78% of the population lives paycheck to paycheck.

This is an extreme amount of pressure to be living under; In this situation, most people are not able to rest even when they fall sick! With these numbers, I am 100% certain that at least some of these people are nice, giving, prayerful people and of those people, I'm sure that a large number of them tithe faithfully at their church.

Overgiving And My Debt

Looking back, I realized that the overemphasis on faith-based giving coupled with a lack of teaching in financial prudence played a large part in holding me back from debt-freedom. Back then, I was ministering in various churches every week, was really focused on getting out of debt, but I was not working full-time.

My father (a pastor) was very particular about not allowing visiting preachers to put pressure on us within my home church. But outside of our church, it was game on. I would attend many services where it was promised that if we give to God, He would give back to us and meet our financial needs. It was sometimes said with a sense of trying to bribe God or twist His arm.

There were times in my journey to debt freedom where God challenged me to give extravagantly out of the little I had, but most of the time, specifically in these services, I didn't check with Abba to see if it was His word *for me*. I simply heard the visiting minister give the promise and I would follow and give whatever I had at that time.

I remember one instance in particular. I had visited a church service in the month of July. The Pastor said that because it was the 7th day of the 7th month of the year, we should give an offering to God in the multiple of 7s. So he started giving at $2,700 and then asked for us to give different multiples down to $700.

He said, "if you do this, God will give you a financial breakthrough in the next 40 days." I was really desperate for this debt to be gone, so I gave the last $2,700 I had that night, expecting God to see my sacrifice and reward it with a breakthrough in the next 40 days. I noted the date in my calendar and waited. And waited. *And waited.*

40 days came and went. Nothing happened at all. This was a wake up call.

I sat before the Lord in my quiet time and asked Him what

happened. I protested, "I gave you my last cent. The pastor said You would give me a breakthrough and You didn't."

God responded, "Did I tell you to give that?" He directed me to Isaiah 61:3 (NKJV): *"For I, the Lord, love justice, I hate robbery for the burnt offering."*

And to Proverbs 3:27-28: *"Do not withhold good from those to whom it is due, when it is in your power to do it. Do not say to your neighbor, "Go, and come back, and tomorrow I will give it," when you have it with you."*

He then showed me that the money in my hands at that time belonged to my creditors and debtors. He was not asking me to give Him money that belonged to someone else. He then asked me to re-read the story of the widow who gave her last mite, which was the story that had motivated me to give in that way.

"And He looked up and saw the rich putting their gifts into the treasury. And He saw a poor widow putting in two small copper coins. And He said, "Truly I say to you, this poor widow put in more than all of them; for they all, out of their surplus put into the offering; but she out of her poverty put in all that she had to live on."
Luke 21:1-4

He highlighted to me that what the widow had put in was her own money. It was the last of what she had, but it wasn't money that was owed to someone else. That night, He told me to stop waiting for a miracle. He told me to study and learn how to become debt free and take the necessary actions that would get me there.

I began to put everything I made outside of my bills directly to my debts and sure enough, there were tons of miracles and favour. This process allowed me to pay off $23,000 in 2 years while working part-time for only 5 months and earning a total of $23,000 in that time. I had loans forgiven, was able to negotiate many of them down, and worked to pay the rest, but the miracles came after I studied what to do and began to apply it.

Short Testimonies Are Not The Full Story

Many of us have heard testimonies of people who have received better jobs, raises, people who are debt free, have paid off their mortgages and so on. Because we are careful to give the glory to God, people who are listening *assume* that in each of these cases, God rained down money on each person.

Sure, sometimes these things happened with extraordinary favour. *But,* most of the time, the person worked in order to receive that blessing. In the church, those who have built wealth may talk primarily about how they gave and sowed throughout the process. In sitting with many of them, giving was just *one of many* wise financial decisions they made in order to become debt and mortgage free with enough assets for their children's children.

Since I started coaching people in changing their financial story, I noticed that the Christians who go through my program will often share how *God* changed their financial situation and call it a miracle. Yes, it may be a miracle that things have changed, but I *also* know that they followed our system and process for owning their workplace value, negotiating that contract well, owning their business worth and paying off that mortgage. In short, they did *their* part.

Often in church culture, we are so focused on the giving aspect (a great lesson), that these people aren't given the time to share the *other* actions they took, a crucial part of the reason for their financial success.

If they were to start teaching on that, it would be presumed as "taking credit" for what God has done. God didn't click send on their emails. He didn't keep their credit card in their wallet when they were tempted to splurge prematurely or buy that new house with the oversized mortgage. They did that by His grace (See 1 Cor 15:10).

Many people who receive phenomenal miracles without learning these lessons also find that the success or blessing is short-lived just like those who win the lottery. Why? Because their mindset has not changed, they end up right where they began and sometimes worse off. Their situation changed temporarily but they did not.

YOU NEED TO PRAY, TITHE AND GIVE

My point is not that you shouldn't pray, tithe or give. I practice these faithfully and firmly believe you *need* to do these three things in order to build wealth. In fact, I believe that a lot of the people who have connected to our company and *Money Mindset SHIFT.* program, after hitting a place of humility and desperately asking God for help, found us as a direct answer to their prayers. I know that the doors that opened to me for my change were not solely dependent on me. They were an answer to my prayers. The favour with people, the connection to the right coaches and even my ability to humble myself and learn when I started this journey were all parts of that bigger puzzle.

There are laws and principles you need to use if you are going to make money work for you, and you need to apply those principles in order to build wealth. Tithing and giving is just one law of money. One of *many*. To focus only on this is to try to bake a cake with just one-quarter of the recipe; it will fall flat every time. What does this mean? It means you need to fill in the gaps and learn what you do not know about money.

SO WHAT DO YOU NEED TO DO?

You need to address these mindsets that have held you back for years. You need to get them out from the root. I'm talking about going from head knowledge to having your heart and subconscious mind in alignment with your financial goals. Then, you need to take inspired, fearless action. You need to commit to learning financial information that is going to help you and reevaluate the information you've heard or been following that has not made a difference. You need to take calculated risks and create a personalized financial plan that will work for you long-term. We'll talk about how to do each of these in the next Chapters.

PART THREE

HOW TO GET UNSTUCK, LIVE DEBT FREE AND BUILD WEALTH

CHAPTER 6

SHIFT The Roadblocks

You CAN change how you think!

— Toyin Crandell

Ihope you had an honest conversation with yourself about the different mindsets you read about in Part 2. As excited as you are to start taking action, if you don't acknowledge the beliefs you have, as much as you may disagree with them in your logical mind, doing more will not make a difference. In order to maximize this process, you must first acknowledge where you are right now in your belief system.

Wrong ideas and mindsets about money are like a virus eating away at your potential, growth and financial freedom. In this Chapter, we are going to talk about the secret weapon to breaking their hold and shifting your financial trajectory.

We will discuss how to remove your money mindset roadblocks.

Now that you've done a thorough job of discovering the limiting beliefs that have been holding you back, you need to actually change your subconscious' responses. Why? So that they stop sabotaging your efforts. How do you do that?

EXPLORE. DEFINE THE ISSUE

Let's use Myth 8: Being Too Broke to Tithe, as our example. You begin by defining exactly what issue you are able to address as well as exploring all the necessary information about that belief.

- Why do you believe that?
- Where did it come from?
- What would happen if you didn't believe that?

EXAMINE. FIND THE ROOTS

Ask the Holy Spirit what He has to say about that belief. What are the ungodly roots?

ESTABLISH NEW THOUGHT PROCESSES

Ask yourself - what is the truth here? What does the bible say about this? Is there any chance that even though I believe this statement, it is not the truth? Begin to have a dialogue with the Holy Spirit about that belief and ask Him for His perspective. Think of some real-life examples of where your mindset roadblock is inconsistent with yours or other people's experience. For instance, how many times have you spent the same amount as your tithe (or more) on emergencies, or other things even while you felt you were broke?

EVALUATE THE CHANGE

After doing the three things above, take a step back and review how much you agree with this belief at this point. Has your mindset changed even slightly? If so, great! If not, continue to have this dialogue with the Holy Spirit asking Him to show you and help you to come into alignment with His perspective.

EXECUTE AND SECURE

When you decide to shift how you are thinking about these mindset roadblocks, you will have to take action in the direction of the truth to help solidify it for your mind. With our example, this can look like talking through the new belief with a friend (who is not limited in their thinking). An active reach would also be deciding to trust and invite God into your financial picture by starting to tithe.

Shifting Out Of Stagnancy

We had a client who was doing extremely well in her business. She received over 5 digits each month, but she knew that something was not right. Her business positively impacted hundreds of families for good, yet for some reason, she had plateaued.

She had become comfortable for years and shifted into maintenance instead of growth. Once we dug into her mindset, we realized that a part of what held her back was the belief that if she changed more people's lives, it would mean an increase in her income and business efforts. She felt the increase in income would distract her from her relationship with Jesus. Because that is her highest priority, she held herself back for years and coasted.

Once we removed that fear and mindset, within 4 weeks her business had a "revival" (her words). She saw massive growth immediately and instead of that growth drawing her away from her love from Christ, she was actually set more on fire to do His work and give extravagantly to His kingdom.

2/3rds Of Her Debt In 2 Months!

I remember a client who did not believe her mindset could be that important in shifting her external financial journey. She had been stuck in debt for years and tried actively to stop overspending, curb her eating out habits and pay off her debt. Nothing worked. The first day she spoke to me, she stated that her goal for debt freedom was to be finished in three years if that was possible. I told her that based on her numbers she could easily get it done in two if we do a thorough work and didn't just focus on the symptoms. She was hesitant but very hopeful and shifted her goal based on my suggestion.

When she started with us, we focused on the biggest leak in her pocket which was overspending at food joints. We dug deeper than a simple budget and helped her to identify exactly what was triggering the habit.

When we found a few different roadblocks that were feeding into it, we began the exercise of shifting those beliefs out of her mindset. Of course over her time with us, we didn't just focus on the Christian beliefs that were holding her back but did a full sweep.

By the time we had completed a few weeks of that exercise, she landed a new, higher paying job. A month after receiving the new job, she got a raise. Yes, you read that right. She got a raise one month after just moving into her position, but she didn't stop there. She was able to make her new income work for her by curbing the spending habit without losing her joy or getting extremely strict with herself. As all these changes took place, she also received money from outside of her workplace.

From these three actions and one miracle, she was able to completely pay off two out of her three debts. She also was able to do something she really enjoyed that year: she went on a road trip and travel excursion with a friend of hers. And guess what she used to cover that trip? Cash. She was no longer traveling on credit. She is now on track to pay off her third debt, so much faster than most people could imagine based on the amount of money she puts toward her debt freedom payments each month.

If you're reading her story and debt is not your challenge. You can apply the same principle to saving up, purchasing that house or putting toward investments.

The "Starving Artist"

I remember speaking to a guy who was adamant about his belief that musicians, especially worship leaders, could not earn a living and build financial freedom in that profession. He bought into the "struggling artist" mindset, hook, line, and sinker. He wanted to shift out of that so that he could use his gifts to glorify God and not run away from his calling, while taking care of his family.

So what did he do? He decided to apply our process for shifting his beliefs. When I asked him, on a scale of 1-10 how much do you agree with this belief (that musicians cannot earn a living and build financial freedom), he responded 11! By the time he completed our full process, his belief in that statement had reduced to a 4 of 10. He told me 24 hours later, that he had done more in the last 24 hours related to his calling and profession than he had done in the previous 5 months.

This is the power of learning how to get your mind working with and not against you in your financial goals.

Let's do a quick review. Here are some of the old ways of trying to shift financially.

- Investing tens of thousands of dollars into getting a Masters or Ph.D. degree. Then, crossing your fingers and hoping that will result in an increase in your income.
- Simply wishing for the best, not thinking about it and believing things will magically get better.
- Focusing all your effort on increasing your income because, "if you could just earn more, you would be financially free."
- Giving yourself every single spending restriction and limitation you can.
- Trying to bribe God by giving Him more than you have to give.
- Stifling the misery you feel inside by claiming to be "blessed and highly favoured," whenever people ask how you are doing.
- Staying up at night thinking and hoping that things will change one day without creating a plan.

Some people try to ignore the fact that they don't have any savings, and they hope things just work out, and it never does.

Some say, "Well if this debt's not getting paid off, I'm just gonna apply for bankruptcy," which has its own consequences.

Some say, "I'm just going to try to please the people around me or present an image that goes with the position I have in my job by overgiving or overspending."

While others go the other extreme of hoarding money and not spending what they have to the point where their children can smell the stench of poverty in their home even though they have thousands in the bank.

Others save, save, save, and have emergencies that eat up all their savings as they go.

Here is the new way of doing things:
- First of all, you need to stop doing what is not working.
- You need to discover your money mindset roadblocks; the fears, the beliefs, the experiences that are causing you to sabotage yourself financially.
- You need to shift those roadblocks out of the way.
- Once you have shifted those beliefs, you must then begin to take inspired, specific action to change your financial reality.

CHAPTER 7

Take Inspired, Fearless Action

If you wish to move mountains tomorrow,
you must start by moving stones today.

— African Proverb

Shifting your mindset is not enough. When you have dealt with the old ways of thinking that have kept you limited, you need to do what most others will not do. You need to take inspired, fearless action. You want to commit to learning and applying financial information that will actually set you up to succeed.

You need to take calculated risks. Create a sure-fire financial strategy that will work long-term for you without burning you out. I've seen too many people willing to learn but unwilling to spend the time required. We want lifelong lessons given to us in "instant coffee" packages. Real, lasting transformation doesn't work that way. James Dobson, Christian author and founder of Focus On The Family once said, "Enthusiasm is no substitute for preparation." Have you prepared yourself for the opportunities God wants to send your way?

Jesus helped most of the people who came to Him. He answered their questions, healed them and set them free from oppression. When it came to His disciples, He gave them everything He had. They walked with Him for three years and afterward, though they were uneducated men, the Sanhedrin, after testing them, seeing their wisdom, boldness, and grace, had to say, "These men have been with Jesus" (Acts 4:13). That wasn't said of Nicodemus though he learned from Jesus.

If this is an area that matters to you and your family, invest the time necessary to learn what you do not know.

What You Do Is More Important Than What You Know

In Myth 9, we discussed the necessity of no longer sitting back and waiting for a miracle. We saw that most of the population in North America, nice and caring as they may be are struggling financially. Not because of a lack of knowing what to do, but because of a persistent habit of self-sabotage where they do not *do* what they *know*.

My father, Amos Dada, has always said: "Wisdom is knowing what to do, skill is knowing how to do it, virtue is getting it done!" It is not enough to acquire new information if you are not willing to apply it and change. Many of you are setting goals in your careers and businesses. You're creating lists and action plans to increase your income or pay off your debt but then you wake up in the morning and realize:

- You forgot to call _____...

- Your desk is FILTHY and needs to be reorganized...
- There are just these "few" emails you haven't yet responded to...
- There is an expense you forgot to include in your budget this month, so your debt payment money has to go there instead…
- "Oh shoot! How long was I just on Instagram?"
- "Why did I come on Facebook again?"

And the infamous, "Oh my goodness, the whole day is done. What happened?"

You want to focus but you continue to run away from your most important tasks and fill your time with things that just don't matter. It's easy to set goals and create action plans but the people who pay off their debt and increase their income do it because they take inspired fearless action.

Distraction is one of the most common symptoms of self-sabotage. It is a crutch that can keep you from fulfilling your greatest dreams. When you have shifted the hidden roadblocks that feed distraction and procrastination, you must then break the habits you have built in the past by taking inspired action.

"Success is not an Egg McMuffin, delivered to us for a $3, three-minute investment. No, success is the Sistine Chapel—it takes years, pain, frustration, thousands of brushes, colors and crumpled up sketches before you have your masterpiece."
Paul Angone

Peter didn't know the water would hold him up when Jesus called him out until he stepped on it. My father, also often says, "They say knowledge is power. It is the *application* of knowledge that produces power." In other words, you can be a very smart dummy.

ADD VALUE TO YOURSELF

The first and most basic lesson I learned from every single millionaire that coached me since I decided to shift out of lack was this: Add value to yourself, commit to sharing that value with those who need it and money will find you. "Value out = cash in."

I initially thought this was the most impractical piece of advice ever *but* as I heard it from men and women who were impacting multitudes of people positively all over the world, people who had never heard each other speak, ran in different circles and across areas of expertise and even continents, I couldn't ignore it.

Instead of staying critical, I understood that there was something they knew that I did not and I followed their directive. I gave myself completely to learning and adding value to myself so that I had something to offer the world.

Let me be clear. When I refer to adding value to yourself, I am *not* speaking of trying to gain some worth that you are missing out on as a human being. *Everyone* has inherent worth. From the moment you were conceived until now, you were and are worth fighting for. You are created in the image of God, loved, treasured and you are valuable beyond description.

When I speak of adding value to yourself, I speak of the value that affects your net worth, income, and relationships. I speak of improving the "you" that interacts with others, contributes to society and navigates the many challenges and joys of life. If you are able to master this one principle of adding value to yourself, you are able to become established in any area or field of study, income stream or strength of character. If you can get a hold of this one principle, you can determine your own financial worth.

You need to be purposeful about investing 1-3 hours every single day adding value to yourself.

If you value your financial freedom enough, begin to read books, watch videos, and find genuine experts who have real-life results to back up their methods. It takes self-discipline. It takes sacrifice and commitment to change something as deeply ingrained as settling for less than what you are capable of. You are not a victim of your mind's thoughts. You can "set your mind on things above" (Colossians 3:2). Fix your thoughts on what is true, and honorable, and right, and pure, and lovely, and admirable. Think about things that are excellent and worthy of praise (Philippians 4:8).

Leadership expert John Maxwell said, "Growth is the only guarantee that tomorrow is going to get better. 99% of people today are assuming - just assuming - that somehow they'll get better. Very sad. Because let me tell you something about assumption. Assumption is a huge disappointment in life. You show me a person that assumes and I'll show you a person that almost daily is disappointed."

Unfortunately, for many Christians, prayer has become an excuse for indecision and inaction. As a finance coach, I speak to and work with people from various religious or areligious backgrounds. I often notice when I speak to someone who is not Christian, they weigh their options. They've been broke, stuck and unhappy for years. They need financial help. They need to increase their income, change their habits so they can have money sitting in the bank and leave a legacy for their children. They are speaking to someone who knows how to help them do this. So, they take action.

In contrast, I'll speak to a believer in Christ who has been praying and fasting for financial breakthrough. They have been begging God to set them free from lack and teach them how to shift into abundance for the sake of their children and future. They see the options and often tell me, "Toyin, this is exactly what I've been praying for. I cried out to God and all of a sudden a friend sent me a link to one of your classes. I'm so grateful to God that I'm speaking to you." Then when offered an opportunity to make a decision and actually begin the journey towards the change they've been praying for, some say, "Let me just pray about it for another week or so." I often don't hear back from them though a few contact me months or years later, worse off than they started, wondering if there is still an opportunity for them to take action.

This is one of the most painful things I have witnessed and one of my driving reasons to write this book specifically for the church. I have seen too many Christians say no to their dream expecting God to magically fix it. They then come back to us after new home refinances, second mortgages, skyrocketing debt, less time and fewer resources than they had when He gave them the initial wake up call.

So make a commitment to yourself to do what it takes to shift. Create a debt freedom and not a debt management plan. Increase your income, working smart, not just working hard. If you have a family, working 3 jobs may end up burning you out more than the financial pressure you feel. If you are running a business, learn how to leverage the tools that are available to you in our generation to make your business profitable. Do not settle for an expensive hobby. Give back from whatever you receive. Fight for your change.

CHAPTER 8

Success Leaves Clues

Formal education will make you a living;
self-education will make you a fortune.

— Jim Rohn

You're probably used to happy-go-lucky financial books that tell you everyone can change or anyone reading this book can do this! I have some real news for you. It takes a certain type of person to achieve the type of transformation we have discussed in this book. I know it because I have been able to observe those who change and many who do not, despite how much they all say they want it.

What distinguishes those who change from those who do is not, is not a matter of their sector, family background, history, current savings amount, years they've known Jesus, skin colour, etc. What distinguishes those who will achieve financial transformation from those who will not is a matter of character. It is what is inside the person. Who you are is more important than what resources you currently have at your disposal.

There is good news. Who you are is a function of who you decide to be. Even if you have been the double-minded, always wavering, non-committed type, God has given you an ability to choose to be someone different. I have noticed that there are three specific traits that separate those who are able to shift and break the cycles of lack or stagnancy, no matter how long they have been there.

TRAIT ONE: COMMITMENT

The people who succeed are 100% committed to their why. They are committed to the dream God has placed inside of them. They know very clearly what their purpose is and they fight for it with everything that they have. They understand that growing financially is never about the money but about the passion, the purpose and the mission God has placed them on this planet for.

I recently spoke to someone who acted like she didn't care about getting better, though she was struggling enough to contact me. She was earning about $2,000/mth, carrying tens of thousands in debt and her family was struggling to meet their basic bills each month. According to her, she was good because she's smart and she can figure it out on her own.

Never mind that this had been her situation for 9 years, she could figure it out on her own. After all, she was studying for an extra qualification that was guaranteed to increase her income. Because we all know that your paper certificate is the guarantee for financial freedom. Right? No.

You can guess it, she was broke. And not just broke in her

bank account. She was broke in her thinking. And that's the saddest type of broke you can ever be. Here's some truth for you: Success does not happen by accident and if you keep on telling yourself that you don't want it, *you will never have it.* If you treat your significant other like you don't want or need them how long will they hang around? Not long. Yet many people want to pretend and justify being financially stuck by saying:

"It's not that bad."

"It could be worse."

"I just want to cover my bills, I don't need anything extra.

"I don't need to save, I'm good just getting by."

"I earn good money. I mean I have nothing to show for it, but I do receive $10k each month so I must be good."

Why do you do this? Because you have not yet become committed to your change. You know you want the help but when you see the light at the end of the tunnel, you park your car in the dark, singing your victim song. You allow the fear of failure, fear of the unknown and the familiar feeling of being "broke" keep you from taking action.

A client once said something in an interview at our annual celebration event, *Our Rising,* that cracked me up! She said that when she was initially faced with the decision to change, her first thought was, "Me and my problem are fine." All her fears had come up in the moment of commitment. All of a sudden, it looked too scary to shift.

Here's the truth - you cannot *afford* to stay where you are! You cannot afford to continue wasting time working for the sake of a paycheck when there is a calling on your life to serve with purpose. You cannot afford to wake up at night thinking about where to move money so things don't bounce. You cannot afford to continue being indebted to slave masters in the name of credit card companies and banks. You cannot afford to end this year looking at how much money you made with nothing to show for it. You cannot afford to allow your children to grow up without learning solid financial principles. It hinders their ability to freely go where God sends them. You cannot afford to be broke any longer!

That client could not afford to be friends with lack any longer. She decided to break her relationship with her problem and her entire *life* was transformed 180 degrees within a matter of weeks.

The people I have watched change their situation are the ones who have become sick and tired of being sick and tired. They are 1000% committed to doing their part in order to see the change they have been praying for. They do not care what it takes (as long as it is legal, ethical and moral), they take hold of the opportunities in front of them and *run with it.*

When you have access to changing your circle, *grab it.* When you have access to someone who is in your corner and 100% about *your* success, *take it!* Financial freedom does not happen by accident. Nobody changes because they "want" to. Everyone "wants" to be carefree about finances. Everyone "wants" to have extra in the bank. Only those who are actually committed to doing the necessary things it will ever get it. The rest are going to continue "wanting" all their lives.

I hope you heard that.

Everyone "wants" debt and financial freedom. Only the committed will get it.

TRAIT TWO: RESOURCEFULNESS

Many people who do not have financial resources feel like they are "behind the game" and that they do not have what they need to change financially. They automatically think that being broke is a liability and use that as a crutch to never come out. The truth is, starting "broke" or with very little often allows you to build a muscle in your character that simply cannot be worked when you have everything handed to you on a silver platter.

That trait is *resourcefulness*. When you are starting with what feels like nothing, it forces you to think more creatively and use your resources more efficiently. You are able to leverage your passion, skills, network like you would not have thought of doing if you have things neatly lined up in a row.

When you start with nothing, you are more likely to be 100% committed to your journey than someone who is lulled into thinking they are in a great place because they're saving $100 a month. In order to achieve the change you have been praying for, you must start right now with what you have.

I remember at the beginning of my journey, I needed to create a webinar for my business and we didn't have the money to purchase professional lights *(or anything else in lieu of a professional studio)*. I relied on natural light from our bedroom window and in that season I also couldn't record in the mornings because I was watching our daughter alone while my husband was in school.

So what did I do? I waited until he got home in the afternoon, gave myself an hour to recuperate from a hectic day with a toddler and set up my laptop on our coffee table. The height was not optimal for recording so we stacked it with a couple of huge bible dictionaries we owned. We had invested about $200 into a microphone set which was a huge improvement from the $50 microphone I used in the very beginning. I had learned that the audio quality mattered much more than the video. Then, I brought in the one lamp we owned in the house put that on the table as well, set up my mic, got everything to face our window and started recording.

Of course, that was also the beginning of my learning how to record webinars, so I was not great at it and had to start all over again a couple of times. By the time I was recording for the third time, I was in a flow. I had gotten about two-thirds of the way through the webinar when I noticed that the worst case scenario was unfolding right before my eyes: the sun was going down!

As I continued to speak, there was a huge shadow cast on my face and the lamp simply was no longer able to cover my full face well enough. As the sun sunk lower and lower in the sky, the bottom half of my face literally started to disappear in the darkness so they could only see from my nose upward while I spoke #blackgirlreality. I made a mental commitment to finish strong because I had attempted this webinar too many times to put it off for another time.

I completed the webinar that way and put it out into the market. It was the best I could do with the very limited resources I had at that time. That webinar earned us tens of thousands of dollars before I remembered how horrible the video quality was to redo it. Until this day, myself and my Executive Assistant have belly laughs when we think about the moment the sun started going down and how I could do nothing about the situation. She saw the whole thing go down. Back then, she was a "friend helping me out" because I was not paying enough to call anyone an Executive Assistant.

Resourcefulness was finding a way to start learning from a real coach when we didn't have enough for food that month. Resourcefulness was hustling and negotiating my debts down when I only earned $23,000 and paid off $23,000 in two years.

People who are resourceful make every reason "they can't" the exact reason they did. They take no excuses and get the work done despite all the challenges and uncontrollable circumstances life throws at them. It's always too early, too late, too little time, too many kids, too much work, too this and too that. There is always an excuse for the uncommitted.

Yet, I have watched people go from uncommitted, "go with the flow", que sera sera attitudes to committed and resourceful and seen them squeeze water out of a rock. They know changing their habits is an upstream battle and are ready to step up to the challenge.

Some people ask me why I expect so much from the people I coach and partner with. It is because I know, for a fact, that we are much more capable than we allow ourselves to believe. While everyone else around us is telling us to take the easy road and wait until the situation is perfect, we know that real change will only happen when you take extreme ownership of your current situation and do whatever it takes to change it.

Trait Three: Humble and Coachable

I used to believe I knew it all. I can't tell you how many times my dad would counsel me in my high school and University days and I thought "He just doesn't understand my situation. These days aren't the same as when he was in University." Today, I am beyond grateful for those mornings he would wake all 5 of us up at 6:00am to teach us life lessons before we headed to school.

It's funny, many of the lessons I share in this book, himself and my mum tried to tell me years earlier during my ministry days. Since I was not coachable in the area of finances, I did not listen. It took God humbling me in bringing us to a place where we had nothing left. It took that experience, for me to consider that maybe, *just maybe*, my dad, a financially free career professional and pastor who was not dependent on a church salary, knew a thing or two about balancing ministry with proper financial planning.

If you are serious about changing your situation, you must be willing to humble yourself and learn. You must empty your cup and recognize that your way is not working. You must commit yourself to learn from the best and applying what you hear.

"Often the most costly advice you can ever get is free. Find masterful mentors and invest in yourself!"

Unknown

In a Google, YouTube and DIY age, many people pose as experts without going through the fire of experiencing what they are teaching and watching it work. Others see a wonderfully written article and assume the information is the "secret sauce" that will change their lives forever. Unfortunately, if learning to break financial mediocrity and build wealth was available on Google and YouTube, 75% of Canadians wouldn't be in debt and 78% of Americans wouldn't lack a basic emergency fund.

What Is The Purpose Of A Mentor?

A mentor does two things for you. They give you new ideas and keep you accountable. As you've read this book, followed the activation points and had honest conversations with yourself, there are new thoughts and ideas that are bouncing around in your head right now. You have new ways of thinking that you would not have discovered if you didn't make the time to sit down and listen to someone else.

A mentor is able to see the bigger picture and open your eyes to that perspective. They are able to direct you on the type of inspired action you need in order to see results in the shortest possible timeline.

I'm going to be completely honest with you, this *one* key changed my life. My first opportunity to work with and learn from a real expert came at the lowest point in our financial journey. It was in the month where we had less than zero for our family. This is the same month I mentioned in Chapter 1 where we contemplated getting food from the food bank because there was nothing in our fridge.

For the longest time, I figured I could do this business and finance thing alone. I am a smart woman, and have accomplished much since my youth but living in that state was my wake up call that I needed help. I remember speaking to my husband about this opportunity and telling him, "Babe, if I could figure this out on my own, I would have done so already. I read a stupendous amount of books, lived in the Google search world, watched over 20 free webinars in the span of a month, purchased various online courses that were cookie cutter, uninvolved streams of passive income for the seller and nothing has changed. I need help!"

When I identified that this coach was committed to understanding where I was starting, giving me specific personalized feedback and had real-life success through his business coaching method, I paid attention. As much as we did not have the means that month to get food, we got resourceful and found the means to work with him. In two months after earning a maximum of $500/month in my business previously, I had my first $7,000 revenue month.

He helped me to set up the basics of a profitable business. Over the years the business has grown and our needs for learning systems from the best has as well. But I will never forget the lesson that very first investment taught me. At the point of writing this book, we have invested over $100,000 on getting the best, of the best in building our business the right way.

The very first time I needed to do this, I felt all sorts of fear. It was my first time investing in my growth outside of my University degree. I decided to switch my thought from, "Will this work for me?" to "How do I make sure this works for me?" and the rest has been history. I am still particular about *who* I learn from, but now, making the decision to invest in myself is a no-brainer because I have seen direct results in my mindset and business with each decision to humble myself and learn from the best.

I have learned that Google, Youtube, free webinars, reading books is *nothing* compared with speaking directly with someone who has been where you are and is now where you are trying to go. Nothing compares to someone who cares enough to know your story, answer your questions and invest time in giving you personalized feedback. Someone who can see exactly what mistakes you are making, and can help you course correct as needed. Someone who knows the pitfalls to avoid and can advise you on small adjustments that will accelerate your process of growth.

Over the years I realized something: every single coach and mentor that I have, have mentors and coaches of their own! My Neuroscience Success Trainer, a published Neuroscientist who spent 20 years studying how to optimize our brain in order to hit our goals recently reminded her students, that she has a mindset coach! Why? Because we are human beings and nobody is exempt from having blind spots.

Don't try to do this alone. Find the best mentor out there for where you are right now and invest whatever it takes to work with them so that you are no longer in the same place month after month, *after month.*

Why? Because success leaves clues.

CHAPTER 9

What Is This Really About?

We will pick up our cross,
We will follow after You,
We'll follow after You...

— Toyin Dada (*Broken Spirit, Contrite Heart* album)

_____

We will be ending our time together with some key distinctions that I want you to remember as you begin to take inspired, fearless action.

1. IT'S ABOUT LIVING FOR THE WILL OF GOD

"Then He said to them, "Beware, and be on your guard against every form of greed; for not even when one has an abundance does his life consist of his possessions." And He told them a parable, saying, "The land of a rich man was very productive. And he began reasoning to himself, saying, What shall I do, since I have no place to store my

crops?' Then he said, 'This is what I will do: I will tear down my barns and build larger ones, and there I will store all my grain and my goods. And I will say to my soul, "Soul, you have many goods laid up for many years to come; take your ease, eat, drink and be merry."' But God said to him, 'You fool! This very night your soul is required of you; and now who will own what you have prepared?' So is the man who stores up treasure for himself, and is not rich toward God."

Luke 12:15-21

God's goal and aim is that we would love and honour Him. He wants to bring us into a state in which we please Him entirely and praise Him in every moment. A state in which He is all in all to us, and where He and we, rejoice continually in the knowledge of His love. It's about Christians rejoicing in the saving love of God, set on us from all eternity and about God rejoicing in our responsive love, drawn out of us by His grace through the gospel.

God's will is that we would come to the saving knowledge of His son Jesus Christ. And not just yourself, but that the entire world would come to repentance. As Jesus said, that everyone who sees His Son and believes in Him would have everlasting life and that Jesus would raise us up on the last day.

God's will is that the heaven and the earth will be united in His Son. It is that His kingdom would be made manifest in this day and age as well as in the age to come. This whole life is about the glory of God in His Son Jesus Christ. Jesus is coming back as our Bridegroom, our King, and our Judge. In the growing darkness, we need to be a church body that is truly willing to learn, change and adapt as He teaches us.

Jesus never used blessings, benefits or perks to entice people to follow him. So the purpose of this book is not to draw you to Christ for the purpose of getting a "better" life. It is to speak to those who have already committed themselves to

Him, to move away from our self-imposed limitations and live out the calling and purposes God has set before us, however that may look.

It is to help you get ready to serve wherever He wants to send you. If you read these principles and try to use them for selfish gain, you will probably have some success, but in light of eternity, it will be completely fruitless.

> *"A person is a fool to store up earthly wealth but not have a rich relationship with God."*
> Luke 12:21 NLT

> *"Blessed are those whose lawless deeds have been forgiven,*
> *And whose sins have been covered.*
> *"Blessed is the man whose sin the Lord will not take into account."*
> Romans 4:7-8

If you do not have a genuine relationship with God through His son Jesus Christ, you need that more than you need a financial breakthrough. You need to be forgiven of your sins and brought into relationship with a God who loves you so much that He died in your place. If that is you, take a moment, put this book aside and pray directly to God. *Repent for your sins, acknowledge Christ as your Lord and Saviour and receive His unfailing love and mercy.*

Please note, when you give your life to Christ it is not a guarantee of wealth or finance. It is a commitment to follow Him *wherever* He leads. I started off in ministry in the context of preaching the gospel on the streets, worship leading, ministering in churches, and teaching Bible studies, then He sent me into business and finance.

At the same time, one of the missionaries we partner with was originally pursuing full-time business as her ministry. He called her out of that to do mission work by sharing the gospel on college campuses. He has a place for each one of us and what matters is our relationship with Him, our willingness to go wherever He sends and be our absolute best wherever that is. Doing God's will is to stop limiting yourself and letting your light shine.

When you focus on and develop your walk with the Lord first, you will learn how to hear His voice and follow Him. Honestly, if you attempt this journey focused only on your profit and comfort, you set yourself up to build your trust and security in money. That is a dangerous place to be. However, when you can tap into the joy of walking in a real relationship with God through His Son Jesus Christ, your desires become His desires. You learn what He is calling you to do in each season.

If He has called you to build wealth to finance the kingdom, He is able to help you balance that with being wholly given to His will. If that is the case for you, when you have gotten out of your stagnancy or lack, take care that you do not become dull because of "the good life". *Push* for the fullness of the knowledge of Christ. No complacency!

Christian brothers and sisters, don't expect poverty or lack. The *Lord* is our Shepherd.

Christian brothers and sisters, don't love or depend on riches. The *Lord* is our Shepherd.

He knows what we have need of and He is a good Father willing to take care of His children.

"Only God enriches life without adding sorrow to it."
Sunday Adelaja.

Remember that money is neutral. It's paper and stones and

all that matters about money is how you use it to honour God.

Rest In The Journey

When you focus on building the mission and purpose God has sent you for, there is peace in your process. This is the ultimate blessing of having Him as your Guide and Leader and not yourself. In Jesus Christ, there is no striving, no drivenness, no anxiety, and no condemnation. Yes, you desire to give Him your life's best offering but it's from a heart that knows you are loved by Him before you ever did one thing. He saw you when you had nothing and has given you all that you now have, to give back to Him. Oh, praise Him!

2. IT'S BIGGER THAN MONEY

This is about changing how you live, changing how you interact with your family, even how you see yourself. One of my clients was a single mom. She was in a relationship at that time, and called me because her boyfriend told her, "You know, I have been waiting for years to get married to you, but you have been drowning financially for as long as I have known you and I can't knowingly walk into financial trouble."

She called me and said, "Toyin, this guy's telling me I need to get my financial act together in the next few months and I haven't been able to do it in over a decade." She was working two jobs plus overtime just to stay afloat. She said, "I'm beyond stressed and even what I earn doing all this work is not helping me."

Within one week of shifting her mindset in so many areas, she landed a new job that paid her double what either of her previous positions did. This gave her a luxury that she had never experienced before time-freedom. She was able to quit the first two positions, work a normal schedule, pay off her debt monthly, but most importantly, spend valuable time with her daughter each evening.

The shift in her finances triggered a shift in her health and many other areas of her life. Her self confidence grew and she was able to reclaim her space, even in her relationships. She spoke to me a few weeks after getting started with us and said, "Toyin, everyone keeps telling me how different I am. They don't know that this change didn't happen by mistake." She was now able to think and focus on the big picture purpose God had placed her here for. She is walking in peace and was able to invest her time and focus on the people that mattered most to her instead of giving every moment to work.

This is about more than money. This is about taking your life back. It is about owning your financial future and making decisions that are going to benefit you, your community and the generations to come.

While writing this book, we were doing our taxes for the previous year and as I reviewed our numbers, they said: balance. We were able to give to charities and non-profit organizations that are saving lives every single day. We were able to enjoy ourselves with things like an all-expense paid, all-inclusive vacation for our family, our parents and a couple of friends. This was a dream come true for us. We were able to re-invest in our business and my own mindset and professional growth.

We also had a solid amount saved specifically for paying taxes. While others resent this, it was a goal of mine. We were able to pay joyfully for the expense of running our business and bless those who worked with us with competitive wages while giving them room to live their purpose as well. We were able to cover all our living expenses, without one second of worry about where it would be coming from. We have already long paid off all of our debts so there were no numbers toward debt freedom payments, a great feeling all in itself. With all this done, we still ended the year with a higher net worth than we had coming in. We did all this while helping hundreds of people pay off almost a million dollars worth of debt, scale their income by hundreds of thousands of dollars and regain peace and order in their financial journey. The year we did this, I only had 4 months of full-time work on the business because I was on bed rest from the miscarriage for two months and I took another 6 months off to focus on a different God-project full-time.

This is the power of pursuing God's purpose and not just money. It becomes a win-win-win situation. A win for our clients and their families, a win for our staff, a win for each of our coaches, a win for our vendors, a win for my community and a win for my family.

More than that, being financially free allows me to focus on my priorities as a wife, a mother, a worship leader and volunteer on different projects that are also in line with my purpose. To be able to take time off my business to be pregnant and have our second child while prioritizing my health. It allows me to serve in my passion and take breaks whenever I want to draw closer to Abba. To literally pause in the middle of all the activity to hear His voice with no pressure to earn. It enables me to take a full day to rest each week, a month's worth of prayer retreats in solitude to grow in the knowledge of Christ each year and come out sharpened and able to serve better.

Being financially free enabled me to take the time to write books that I wouldn't have had the presence of mind to write were I frantically trying to think of how to pay our bills. It allows me to serve people and help them make wise decisions that release them into their God-given destiny.

Being financially free is not about the money. It's about

being able to lay up treasures in heaven, where it counts. Where the stock market can't affect it. It's about being free to go where God sends us when He sends us without having to think about whether our kids will have food to eat. Sure, for some people maybe that's the exact challenge He wants them to have? I am not a theologian and won't pretend to know all there is about God. But I do know that this has allowed us to focus on the actual work He sends us for when He sends us there.

Your financial freedom is not only for you. It's for your family. It's for your church, non-profits and the people they impact.

It's for tens, hundreds, thousands and millions of other people that will be blessed by your abundance.

CONCLUSION

Your Next Steps

In Part 1 of this book, I explained just how influential your mindset has been in creating your current financial reality. Simply put, what is happening between your two ears will have a greater effect on your bank account than any external action you are trying to take.

We addressed how to stop making bad financial decisions that lead to overspending, underearning, and sabotaging your financial goals, even if you've tried and failed in the past. We explored how to have a clear financial plan for hitting goals, whether that's buying a house, becoming debt free, having a solid retirement fund, or becoming financially free. We examined how you are able to travel where you want, get the things you've waited for years for without feeling guilty about spending that money afterward. We talked about how to take control of your finances and shift from living paycheck to paycheck to having money in the bank. We covered how to do all of this without working a crazy amount of overtime, changing careers, starting from scratch, or putting yourself on such a strict budget that you're not able to live at all.

In Part Two of this book, we addressed 9 specific myths, mindsets that particularly affect Christians and keep them stuck in patterns of financial lack and stagnancy. I hope you spent time reviewing that section over and over to examine your mindset and beliefs.

So what do you need to win? You need to stop doing or focusing on what is not working. You need to discover your money mindset roadblocks. You need to remove those money mindsets that are causing you to self-sabotage. You need to stop waiting for a miracle and take inspired action. You need to invest in a great mentor or coach. These shifts alone are enough to propel you into consistent financial abundance.

Now you have a choice. You can either take all the information I've just given you and forget all about it. You can continue to pray and wait for the financial breakthrough to fall on your lap, work yourself sick, live paycheck to paycheck, staying up at night wondering where on earth your money is going, and why things aren't working for you no matter what you try.

You can allow your kids to grow up watching you and learning how to duplicate your current frustration, or you can be the person that completely changes your family's story.

You can begin to live a life of more than enough while remaining humble, grateful and obedient to God every step of the way. You can learn how to shift your mindset to increase your income, your savings and investments without the struggle and have more than enough to cover the things that you need and the things that you want.

Here's How We Can Help

As I mentioned, many people have invested their wisdom and time into my success and I am committed to doing the same for others. My mission is to bring 1 million people out of financial lack or stagnancy and into a place of thriving and an ability to live out the mission God has given them. My mission is to see them give back and positively impact their communities, churches and kingdom projects.

Now, I know that there are others who are exactly where

I used to be. You are *hungry* for change. You will do whatever that requires of you in integrity and morality. You are ready for abundance and will not wait one more day, month or year to shift. While others run away from discomfort and growth, you choose to run *towards* it. You know that your life will be richer for it and have simply been waiting for the path to take.

You know that it's not comfortable to choose to change the trajectory of your life from stuck, mediocre and "just getting by" to a life that can leave a legacy. You are looking at coming generations and want to give them something to be grateful for from your journey.

We are blessed to have multiple classes, retreats and one primary program through which we walk with those who are committed to their change in a focused way. By the grace of God, I have been able to assist thousands in walking into their shift. They've paid off almost a million dollars worth of debt within 3 years and increased their income by hundreds of thousands of dollars. This is only from reported numbers, not including those who have seen the impact but have not informed our team.

I invite you to visit **www.toyindada.com** and join my next free online masterclass. At the end of it, I will share a link through which you can book a call with a member of my team so that we can speak to you personally about applying these principles to your mind, and to your finances starting today. Whatever your biggest challenges are, we've seen it, and we know how to overcome them.

We will get on the phone for about 45 minutes, and in this free session, we will craft a step-by-step game plan to completely change your relationship with and use of money. We show you how you can make money work for you by increasing your savings, investing, paying off debt (if you have any) and shifting your finances out of stagnancy. We will help you to get clear on what has been keeping you personally stuck, tackle the top three money beliefs that are holding you back (they may not be related to the 9 listed within this book). We also help you figure out where you want to be financially, and how to to get there.

If we are a fit you *may* be invited into our 8-week program, *Money Mindset SHIFT.* This is where we help people shift into the fullness of God's purpose for their business, career and overall finances. Every single person who has been through our program has identified it as a marked moment of change in their lives. If we are not a fit, you will receive personalized recommendations for what your next steps should be.

Finally, I'll say this, people are rewarded in public for what they have practiced for years in private. Stop focusing on your image and begin focusing on your change today.

I would like to personally congratulate you for investing in yourself by reading and applying the lessons in this book. I pray that God's perfect will for your life is established and that you prosper in all things as your soul prospers.

To your financial freedom,

Toyin Crandell

Psalm 112

Prosperity of the One Who Fears the Lord.

Praise the Lord!
How blessed is the man who fears the Lord,
Who greatly delights in His commandments.
His descendants will be mighty on earth;
The generation of the upright will be blessed.
Wealth and riches are in his house,
And his righteousness endures forever.
Light arises in the darkness for the upright;
He is gracious and compassionate and righteous.
It is well with the man who is gracious and lends;
He will maintain his cause in judgment.
For he will never be shaken;
The righteous will be remembered forever.
He will not fear evil tidings;
His heart is steadfast, trusting in the Lord.
His heart is upheld, he will not fear,
Until he looks with satisfaction on his adversaries.
He has given freely to the poor,
His righteousness endures forever;
His horn will be exalted in honor.
The wicked will see it and be vexed,
He will gnash his teeth and melt away;
The desire of the wicked will perish.

LET'S HAVE THE CONVERSATION

One reason many Christians remain stuck in negative financial patterns is that there has been so much fear and taboo around having thought out conversations about money in Christian circles. We've been content to speak platitudes with one another without addressing specific actions needed to shift.

The focus of this book has been to address some of the fundamental reasons we sabotage ourselves as Christians in our various sectors of work. We have been able to identify the most common mindsets and thought patterns that keep Christians stuck, the effect of those mindsets and exactly how to shift them from your mind.

To this end, I would like to challenge you to share this message of addressing these mindsets that have held us back from the full potential God has created us for. Get the message of this book out to as many people as you can. Commit to telling at least fifty of your family, friends, church family and leaders about it or consider getting the book for them as a life-changing gift.

I promise you, as miraculous as changing your family's financial trajectory is, doing it along with your friends and extended church family is an extraordinary blessing that can not be quantified.

My goal is that through each book, each breakthrough session, each *Money Mindset SHIFT.* program cycle, we help 1 million people become financial pillars for the kingdom of God. I ask you to support me in making this mission a reality.

Thank you,

Toyin C.

ACKNOWLEDGEMENTS

I would like to thank my husband Joshua Crandell for his patience, wisdom and consistent support over the years of our friendship and marriage. Babe, the last 12 years have been a thriller suspense movie but this marriage has been a rock and place of safety, laughter, and peace through it all. Second, to my salvation, you are God's best gift to me. Thank you.

Thank you to Taryn-Lee Dube for your unwavering support and hard work in our coaching practice. Your world-class administrative expertise, relational and mindset coaching ability, and belief in our mission have made it possible for us to change thousands of lives.

Thank you to Aunty Bola, Dara, and Ade for your support over the years and for taking us into your homes when we needed a place to stay. Thank you to Jolene for receiving us into your home even though you did not know our names and had only spoken to us twice! You were an angel sent to us that evening in the IHOPU parking lot.

Thank you to the CAC Bethel Toronto and LifeBridge Thamesville family for your support in every single adventure we have taken. You are truly my Christ family.

Thank you to my parents, Amos and Eyitayo Dada for your wisdom and patience with me in this journey. I laugh thinking about all the times you woke my sisters and I up at 6:00 am to lecture us on how to honour God with our lives. I initially despised being woken up so early but now, I teach others what you have taught me. Thank you.

Thank you to mum and dad Crandell for leaving the beauty of Nanaimo, BC, and moving over a thousand miles, to live close by because you believed in our dream and wanted to help us make it happen.

Thank you to my four sisters, two sisters-in-law and two brothers-in-law - Dara and Ade, Ife, Tobi, Debbie, Jason and Melissa, Nick and Vicky and all the many children we've been blessed with. What a blessing it is to be a part of such a large, joyful and unified family!

Thank you to the Jeremiah House Publishing team for your help converting my lived experience and many speaking engagements into a beautifully crafted, published book.

Thank you to Chris-Ann Manning-Forde for your excellent work copy and content editing this project. You are a gift and a friend.

Thank you to Eyitayo and Debbie Dada, Steffany and Gabriella Kerr, Hannah Umukoro and Sharon Edghill for also assisting with this project.

I believe that many families will shift from struggle and stagnation to abundance and significance because of your collective efforts.

God bless you family.

ABOUT THE AUTHOR

Using the principles she teaches, Toyin Crandell went from stuck in tens of thousands of debt, having no food for her family to a multiple 6 figure income. She has helped clients pay off almost a million dollars in debt, and increase their net worth by hundreds of thousands of dollars, all within 3 years.

She is the CEO of Toyin Crandell Coaching, a certified Neuroscience Coach and a Dave Ramsey Solutions Master Financial Coach. She is a high-performance mindset and finance coach and speaker, specializing in helping people increase their income, live debt free, and build wealth in order to positively impact the world.

Her mission is to empower 1 million people in creating a long-term financial shift that allows them to live the life they were created for and transform their families and communities.

She lives with her husband and daughter in Ridgetown, Ontario.

To contact Toyin Crandell for speaking
engagements or order more copies of
Money Mindset SHIFT. *Church Edition:* The Top 9
Myths That Keep Christians Stuck Financially and How To
Get Unstuck, Live Debt Free and Build Wealth!,
visit www.toyindada.com

Facebook: @ToyinDadaFanPage
Instagram: @ToyinDada

Other Titles From Jeremiah House Publishing Available on Amazon

The Squirrel and The Oak Tree - Joshua Crandell
The Squirrel & The Oak Tree is a Canadian folk tale that helps children ages 4-8 learn about values like trust, openness and how to overcome stereotypes and develop friendships with people who are different. Join a quick-tempered squirrel and a wise old crow as they discover an uncommon friendship and learn that: "Things are not always what they seem to be, and sometimes we miss what others can see."

Making Your Marriage Work, Maama's Practical Wisdom For A Lasting, Happy Marriage - Eyitayo Dada
Marriage is not meant to be endured, it is meant to be enjoyed. Too many couples are either bored or holding on "for God's sake" or "for the sake of their children". With practical advice based in the word of God, this book will help revive the joy, passion and laughter in your marriage.

Lily Among Thorns - Mia Christine
lily among thorns gives creative guidance to finding contentment in a world of never enough. For every heart overwhelmed with disappointment, difficulty and the uncertainty of life, these poems, songs, and short stories trumpet bold statements for resilient living, leading the unsatisfied into lasting joy and freedom.

Awaken My Heart: *Listening For The Still Small Voice* - Julia McDonald
Follow Julia on her journey through the Psalms and Proverbs, as she shares lessons from her personal devotionals and then, begin your own! Fill the pages with your own prayers and insights as you search for God in the scriptures. Today is the day for your heart to be awakened to a more intimate relationship with God!

Albums Featuring Toyin Crandell
Available on iTunes, Spotify and CDBaby

Declaration of Dependence - Toyin Crandell
Resonating with soul/jazz vocals and blues-gospel influences, "Declaration of Dependence" gives voice to the dark night of the soul - where God's presence and promises seem most distant - while revealing the comfort, joy and strength found in Christ.

Broken Spirit, Contrite Heart - Toyin Dada
The devoted, the disillusioned and everyone in between converge at the fundamental desire to experience true, pure love. "Broken Spirit, Contrite Heart" is that access point between listener and the personhood of Jesus Christ, unveiling the beauty and depth of His love - a worship experience both refreshing and liberating for any individual with an open ear.

Sparrow - Joshua Crandell
Sparrow's unique blend of R&B, easy listening and jazz highlights encourages listeners to live in patience, peace, and confident trust in the faithfulness of God.

Living Out Love - The Love Movement 4:16
Living Out Love captures the journey of following Jesus Christ through a dynamic mix of soothing acoustic rhythms and catchy electro pop riffs. Jesus' life example ignites our hearts to respond in radical love, faith, and obedience.

Love Letters - Toyin Dada
With its multi-generational sounds and distinctive vocals, Toyin Dada's debut album "Love Letters' succeeds in capturing the unique dynamics of the love relationship between a fiery God and His beloved creation.

Made in the USA
Las Vegas, NV
10 January 2022

41064514R00115